SEVEN DAYS FROM SUNDAY

Books by Tom Galt

SEVEN DAYS FROM SUNDAY

PETER ZENGER: FIGHTER FOR FREEDOM

HOW THE UNITED NATIONS WORKS

VOLCANO

SEVEN DAYS
FROM
SUNDAY

By TOM GALT

Illustrated by Don Freeman

NEW YORK
THOMAS Y. CROWELL COMPANY

Contents

Who Named the Days
of the Week?

Lots of people think they know why a week has seven days, but some might be surprised if they heard how long ago the first weeks were really made. Our kind of week was invented for a special reason, and names were given to the days by men whose purpose has been almost forgotten.

Does all the world have the same sort of weeks?

Well, yes and no.

In a little village in the forest in west Africa every fourth day is a holiday. People gather in the market place that afternoon to buy (and to sell) food, clothes, tools. Someone buys perhaps a beaten copper necklace, someone else a pair of sandals, the soles cut from an old automobile tire. That evening the villagers sing and dance to the sound of drums. Many play games. It is their weekend. But it comes every fourth day.

Next morning before dawn some of the tool or sandal peddlers start walking along the shady forest paths to another village. Market day is different in each place—on purpose. A man who sells necklaces or saws or heavy long-handled hoes can be in one town on its market day, in another the next day, which is market day there, and in a third village the following morning in time for its market day. If he plans his trips carefully, every village is having Saturday when he arrives. For him every day can be Saturday as long as he lives.

Market days in other parts of the world have come every third day or every fifth, sixth, eighth, or tenth day.

But now all big nations—including China and Japan —use our week of seven days, with Saturday the same for us all.

Yet weeks are not natural.

Years are natural. If people forgot what season of the year they were in, they could find out. Long ago they discovered that the sun rose at a different spot along the eastern horizon each morning, some days farther to the right, other days farther to the left, according to the season. In spring as the weather became milder, the sun crept to the left along the eastern horizon morning after morning. Finally one warm dawn the hunters looking from their huts saw that it had stopped shifting and was rising in the same spot as the day before. The solstice had arrived (that word means "the sun stops"). Spring was ended and summer had begun. Next day the sun would rise a little to the right of that spot.

To mark that spot and the season, and to avoid arguments, the ancient Britons built the temple of Stonehenge with its entrance aimed exactly at where the sun

would rise on the day of the summer solstice (in June). This building became their calendar. Their cousins at Carnac in northern France set up a circle of huge stones, and the Egyptians far to the south built their grand temple of Karnak, each facing the sunrise on that day. The Chinese aimed a temple at the sunrise on the winter solstice (in December).

These early people measured months by the moon. Anybody can see when the moon is full and when it is becoming small again.

But you cannot find out the day of the week by looking at the moon or at the place where the sun rises. You can find out the day of the week only by asking someone who has kept track by writing down the days on a calendar. And he learned by asking someone before him.

We know the Bible says God created the world in six days, and on the seventh day he rested. That seems like a good reason for our having weeks, with six workdays and one holiday. But that story implies that weeks had been going on before the Bible was written. And the Bible never mentions any day by name. (There is a good reason why not.)

Then who started the week and gave the days their names?

The days of the week first got their names in ancient Babylonia. And they were named by stargazers.

The Discovery of the Seven Planets

Babylonia was a fairly flat country. Between its two slow rivers (Tigris and Euphrates) farmers planted wheat and vegetables in the muddy fields. From the little hills men wearing tall hats and long robes could look out for miles around. Also the air was rather dry.

In such a country the stars were very clear. In fact, those people could often see the planet Venus even in the daytime.

Crops, as anyone could see, grew with the help of sun and rain from the sky—or withered under too much sun. Sometimes the wheat and vegetables were destroyed by storms of wind or by floods when the rivers rose from too

much rain. And the rains often came when certain constellations of stars were overhead.

Looking at the sky, from which comes so much good
and evil, people asked, "What is in the sky? What forces
are at work there?" And the answer to these questions was
largely mystery. Naturally some of those farmers began
to find their religion in the powers of heaven.

As most people were too busy (or too lazy) to keep
track of the star motions every night, it was the priests
who took up this job. Soon they became very useful by
predicting the best times for planting and for the harvest.

More than six thousand years ago they made some important discoveries.

If you watch the heavens in the evening you will see, as
they did, that the whole dome moves. In one hour some
stars rise in the east, others go down in the west. They
keep moving all night.

I mean, of course, they seem to. Your science books
will tell you that the earth turns, while the sky stays still.
But we should not let our science books make us forget
how the sky looks. If you cannot talk about how things
look, you become like a person who is blind.

So it is good for us to read about ancient astronomy
and remind ourselves of how the glittering vault of evening looks.

The ancient stargazers discovered something more. If
you notice carefully just where the constellations are at

9 o'clock tonight and where they are at 9 o'clock every night, you will see that they shift slowly during a month.

For instance, watch a group of stars that at 9 P.M. is straight overhead. A month later it has slipped westward. After three months (at 9 P.M.) those same stars are near the horizon. Keep watching. Soon they are out of sight. After nine months you will see them (at 9 P.M.) in the east. And at the end of one year from the time you began, that same group of stars (at 9 P.M.) is again straight overhead.

Almost all the stars move around together. So they are called the fixed stars. They stay in the same fixed positions in relation to one another. (Of course, with big modern telescopes we have found out that some are not entirely fixed. They shift a little, very slowly. But the ancient people had no telescopes.)

The priests in Babylonia, Arabia, and Egypt were excited by the discovery that all the fixed stars seemed to travel together, going the whole way round in approximately 365 days.

In Egypt the stargazers worked up a new calendar of twelve months making 365 days in a year. In the year 4241 B.C. the Pharaoh decreed that this would be the official calendar of Egypt.

The priests and poets of Arabia made a different use of this knowledge. They reasoned that if most of the stars seemed to be fixed together, three heavenly bodies evidently wandered among them—the moon, the sun, and one other.

The moon moves quickly. They might see the half moon high overhead at sunset. Seven days later, at sunset, they saw the full moon on the eastern horizon. Counting only where it was seen each evening at sunset, it had gone all the way from high overhead down to the eastern horizon in seven days. In that short time the fixed stars had moved much less—and in the opposite direction.

When they thought of it, they realized that the sun also is independent. Every night at sunset it is in the same place, while the fixed stars have moved.

And those ancient stargazers of Arabia discovered that the beautiful evening star, too, shining so brightly, moves differently from the fixed stars. Gradually they found that it does not circle evenly like the moon but slides on what looks like a strange, looping path of its own.

They had long worshiped the sun and the moon. Adding the evening star to their religion, the Arab priests made a cult of the heavenly three. It was the ancestor of the cult that gave us our week.

Also those Arabs went on the warpath, fought their way into Babylonia, and settled there on the fertile river banks.

As the centuries have moved ahead, religions often have changed, and theirs met special causes for it to expand. In the first place, the Babylonians, with whom they settled, had many other gods. But, in the second place, what really altered this cult of the heavenly three was what the priests found in the sky.

For the Babylonians were star-watchers, too. By the reign of King Sargon of Akkad in 3800 B.C. the writings show that the Babylonian priests had already been expert astronomers for a long time.

Gradually they made another discovery. This took centuries, but when they got it, it was very exciting. They found that seven of the sky's inhabitants wander. The sacred three—the sun, moon, and evening star—were not the only ones. Four others moved independently too.

With our telescopes we have discovered more planets. But the sun, the moon, and the five nearest planets were the only wanderers known in ancient times. However, as the Greek word *planet* means "wanderer," the sun and moon used to be called that; so the ancient people spoke of the "seven planets," including the sun and the moon.

How the Sacred Seven Became the Week

To find all seven took patience and effort. And the men who accomplished it were so deeply impressed by the discovery that they decided to adopt these strange heavenly bodies into their religion.

9

So the cult of the sun, moon, and evening star was expanded. The priests told the king that the sky contained not three but seven wanderers. And they gave them the names of seven gods:

Babylonian name	English name
SIN	MOON
NEBO	MERCURY
ISHTAR	VENUS
SHAMASH	SUN
NERGAL	MARS
MARDUK	JUPITER
NINURTA	SATURN

These were old gods, some of whom had been thought to live on mountains and now were placed in the sky. Later the days of our week were named for them.

This religion was tolerant. Each city developed a different version of it. In Babylon the great god Marduk was supreme. He had created the world. The other six were his councilors. In some cities Shamash was the most important, because the sun is the source of our life. But in Ur the moon god, Sin, was supreme. And in Nineveh the people worshiped especially the goddess Ishtar, the great mother, queen of love, of marriage, and of farms.

Each city had its own stories of these gods, with different ideas about who was the father of whom. As the king of Babylonia ruled over more than twenty of these

ISHTAR

cities, he found it convenient to accept all the stories.
Anyway, their differences did not matter. In fact, many
of the wiser people believed that these seven gods and all
the other gods were really only names for what is divine
in Nature.

As it was in some ways a very good religion, many of
its prayers are beautiful. In a temple the people chanted
to the Moon god:

"When thy word echoest in heaven, all the angels
   of heaven cast themselves before thee in worship.
When thy word roareth above the storm wind, it
   causeth food and drink to flourish.
Thy word maketh fat the stable and the barn. It
   increaseth the creatures of life."

On another day they said:

"Who feareth not his god is cut off like a reed.
Who honoreth not the goddess Ishtar, his limbs rot
   away.
Like the stars of heaven he disappeareth.
Like the waters of the night he melteth away."

And when a man was in trouble he could pray humbly:

"To my merciful god I turn, seeking aid and sighing.
With tears I clasp the feet of my goddess.
O Lord, overthrow not thy servant;
Grasp his hand when he has fallen into the water.
Turn into grace the sin which I have committed.
May the wind bear away the misdeeds which I have
   done.
Tear like a cloth my many evils.
O thou, who rulest all things and steerest mankind,
How gracious is thy mercy, which despiseth not the
   sighing of sinners!"

For this religion temples were built, some of them large and beautiful. Many had towers seven stories high, painted in different colors, one story for each planet. Every clear night the priests climbed the towers and looked at the stars.

For a long while the Babylonians had counted time by moon months. On the day of the full moon they had big celebrations. (Doesn't the full moon sometimes make you feel like celebrating?) On the day of the new moon, and in some places on the day of the growing half moon, too, smaller feasts were held. (The moon was smaller; so naturally the feasts would be smaller.)

If you notice when these phases occur, you will find that they arrive every seven or eight days. So the moon made irregular weeks.

Then some of the priests became enthusiastic about the seven planets and decided that all weeks must have seven days. The day of the new moon was the first of the month. They made it also the first day of a week. The growing half moon was the eighth day. It became the first day of another week. Full moon was celebrated on the fifteenth, which became the first day of the third week. That made the fourth week begin on the twenty-second of the month, within a day or two of the time of the waning half moon.

The waning half moon shines only in the middle of the night when most people are in bed, so they were not bothered by the fact that the first day of the fourth week missed it by a day or two.

While the first of each week was a day of celebration, they had a strange feeling about the other end of the week, the seventh day. It seemed to worry them.

About 2300 B.C. a chronicle of the city of Lagash said, "On the seventh day no one was struck with the whip. The mother corrected not her child. The householder, the overseer, the laborer—the work of their hands ceased.

14

In the graves of the city no corpse was buried. The temple musician played no psalm, uttered no dirge. The wailing women let no lament be heard. In the domain of Lagash no man who had a lawsuit went to the Hall of Justice."

In a law code we find this: "The seventh day is a day of fast for the god Marduk and for his wife, Sarpanitu. On this day the shepherd shall not change his body clothing; he shall not be clad in white; he shall not offer a sacrifice; he shall not talk victoriously. The king must not drive a chariot. He must not issue royal decrees. The seer shall not declare the omens in the sacred place. A physician shall not touch a sick man. It is not suitable to make a wish."

It was not a day of prayer, like our Sunday. It was a day of rest, an unlucky day with many taboos. It was the ancestor of our Saturday.

But at that time the seven-day week was still incomplete in two respects.

First, it did not keep going. After each fourth week they left one or two extra days before beginning another, which had to start on the day of the new moon. Because of the way the moon changes, some months had thirty days, others twenty-nine. As four weeks fill only twenty-eight days, one or two extra days were always left over at the end of a month.

The other thing that was lacking was regular names

for the days. Some people did not give them any names; others did. Each big city in the kingdom had its own main temple and its own priests. They took the planets so seriously that they said each day was ruled by one. But every group of priests had its own list of the seven planets, and each city was very tolerant of the others, who arranged the planets in a different order; so they never even tried to agree. The day of Shamash was followed by Sin and then Marduk in one city. In another city the days went Sin, Shamash, Nebo, etc.

The king found it easier simply to count the days one, two, three, and so on through a whole month. So in Babylonia the seven-day week with named days never became official. It was used by priests, differently in different cities.

Then how did we get the days of the week in a definite order?

How the Days of Our Week Were Named

We got our week from the astrologers. They worked up a very clever system of magic.

They said that all the stars and especially the planets sent down a strange fluid called "influence," which guided people's lives. Therefore if you knew the exact day of the week, month, and year when you were born and the exact day on which you wanted to fight a battle or choose a wife, the astrologers would tell you whether the heavens made this a lucky or unlucky day for you. They would figure out the positions of the stars on those days and also the influences of the planets who ruled those two days. A planet ruled a day by having it named for him or her. And for this the astrologers needed a week of their own—preferably with the days arranged in an order that no one but astrologers could understand.

Gradually the cult became so complicated that only a very learned student of it, who charged high prices for his services, could possibly figure out the effect of all the influences on any one occasion.

Some time before 650 B.C. the astrologers named the days of our week. To do it they first named the hours. If the exact hour of your birth and the exact hour of a battle were important, that would help to make the system more complicated and the services of the astrologers more expensive.

The early Babylonians had had no hours. But, because they counted by sixes, they had divided the day into six watches, just as sailors still do: three watches from sunrise to sunset, three more during the night. However, for businessmen who wanted to make several appointments in a day, a watch was too long; and the Babylonians were great businessmen. So they eventually made six watches by daylight and six in the night, or twelve altogether.

Since the astrologers wanted to be different and mysterious, they imported the Egyptian system: twelve hours by day and twelve by night. That is how we got our twenty-four-hour day. In Babylon the hour was divided into sixty minutes and the minute into sixty seconds. Eventually the Babylonians spoke of a circle as an hour and divided the circle into sixty minutes, or 360 degrees. We do all these things because we learned them from the Babylonians.

By means of the Egyptian water clock they were able to measure these hours. When the clock had run one hour they rang a bell once (as we still do). When it had gone another hour, they rang the bell twice. The night had twelve hours. So the bell rang twelve at dawn. Then they began the hours of daytime.

Later the Hebrews used this same way of numbering the hours. So when you read in the Bible that something happened "at the third hour of day," that means 9 A.M. (Look at our table on page 20.)

But the astrologers went further. They *named* all the hours. Their method of naming the days because of the hours was so ingenious that it really is fun. It worked this way:

Beginning with the slowest planet, which they thought must be the highest, they arranged the planets in order. Actually this is the correct order for the sun, moon, and planets according to their speed, as seen by men:

18

NINURTA	(SATURN)
MARDUK	(JUPITER)
NERGAL	(MARS)
SHAMASH	(SUN)
ISHTAR	(VENUS)
NEBO	(MERCURY)
SIN	(MOON)

And then repeat:

NINURTA	(SATURN)
MARDUK	(JUPITER)
NERGAL	(MARS)
SHAMASH	(SUN)
ISHTAR	(VENUS)
NEBO	(MERCURY)
SIN	(MOON)

and so on, over and over.

To name the hours, they began with the sun. That was the most important of the seven wanderers. To us it still is the most important.

And when they came to the end of one day, they began the next day with whichever planet came next on their list. If one day ended with Nebo (Mercury) the next day began with Sin (the moon).

And so they kept going for seven days, all different. In the tables on the following pages we have used the English names.

NAMES OF BABYLONIAN HOURS

MODERN	HOUR BABYLONIAN	1st DAY	2nd DAY	3rd DAY
NIGHT				
7 P.M.	1	Sun	Moon	Mars
8	2	Venus	Saturn	Sun
9	3	Mercury	Jupiter	Venus
10	4	Moon	Mars	Mercury
11	5	Saturn	Sun	Moon
12 Midnight	6	Jupiter	Venus	Saturn
1 A.M.	7	Mars	Mercury	Jupiter
2	8	Sun	Moon	Mars
3	9	Venus	Saturn	Sun
4	10	Mercury	Jupiter	Venus
5	11	Moon	Mars	Mercury
6	12	Saturn	Sun	Moon
DAY				
7 A.M.	1	Jupiter	Venus	Saturn
8	2	Mars	Mercury	Jupiter
9	3	Sun	Moon	Mars
10	4	Venus	Saturn	Sun
11	5	Mercury	Jupiter	Venus
12 Noon	6	Moon	Mars	Mercury
1 P.M.	7	Saturn	Sun	Moon
2	8	Jupiter	Venus	Saturn
3	9	Mars	Mercury	Jupiter
4	10	Sun	Moon	Mars
5	11	Venus	Saturn	Sun
6	12	Mercury	Jupiter	Venus

4th DAY	5th DAY	6th DAY	7th DAY
Mercury	Jupiter	Venus	Saturn
Moon	Mars	Mercury	Jupiter
Saturn	Sun	Moon	Mars
Jupiter	Venus	Saturn	Sun
Mars	Mercury	Jupiter	Venus
Sun	Moon	Mars	Mercury
Venus	Saturn	Sun	Moon
Mercury	Jupiter	Venus	Saturn
Moon	Mars	Mercury	Jupiter
Saturn	Sun	Moon	Mars
Jupiter	Venus	Saturn	Sun
Mars	Mercury	Jupiter	Venus
Sun	Moon	Mars	Mercury
Venus	Saturn	Sun	Moon
Mercury	Jupiter	Venus	Saturn
Moon	Mars	Mercury	Jupiter
Saturn	Sun	Moon	Mars
Jupiter	Venus	Saturn	Sun
Mars	Mercury	Jupiter	Venus
Sun	Moon	Mars	Mercury
Venus	Saturn	Sun	Moon
Mercury	Jupiter	Venus	Saturn
Moon	Mars	Mercury	Jupiter
Saturn	Sun	Moon	Mars

Each day was then named for the planet that "ruled" its first hour:

Babylonian name	English name of planet	English name of the day
SHAMASH	SUN	SUNDAY
SIN	MOON	MONDAY
NERGAL	MARS	TUESDAY
NEBO	MERCURY	WEDNESDAY
MARDUK	JUPITER	THURSDAY
ISHTAR	VENUS	FRIDAY
NINURTA	SATURN	SATURDAY

It may sound crazy, but that is how our names of the days of the week began.

Also, this system could not retain the old custom of leaving an extra day or two at the end of each month and then beginning a new week on the first of the next month. If a day or two were left over at the end of a month, that magic sequence of named hours would fall apart. Astrologers who really *believed* the new system could not allow any blank, nameless days. So they began counting the weeks one after another straight along, not stopping at the end of each month. And now these weeks have followed one after another without a break for over 2,600 years.

To the king, these astrologers were just one more sect among many. He often consulted them but never made their weeks official. In fact, they kept their system of weeks partly secret.

Who told that secret openly all across Europe? Not the Hebrews. Not the early Christians. Not the astrologers themselves.

The week was carried west by a group of people who are not often spoken of nowadays.

SHAMASH

How the Week Went West

THE BIBLE tells how the Hebrews were conquered by a Babylonian army. The people of Jerusalem heard the beat of hoofs, the squeak of chariot wheels, the unfamiliar shouts of the eastern soldiers. Soon the foreign warriors' peaked helmets were gleaming in the streets. With loud knocks on every door, they demanded bluntly, "Who lives here?"

Only the Hebrew government officials, the business-men, and the rabbis and students were arrested. Thousands of these were led away in captivity. They were marched to a great, sprawling, easy-going city on the Euphrates River.

From 597 to 538 B.C. these Hebrews planted crops, traded, and tried to earn their living in Babylon. Some studied in the huge library.

Here in their time of sorrow they collected the stories and wisdom that we find in the book of Genesis. They pieced it together largely from old documents which they either had with them or found in the Babylonian library. Here, too, the great prophet Isaiah wrote some of his best poems and prayers.

When the Hebrew leaders returned to Palestine after their captivity, they believed strongly in the seven-day week. They now had the book of Genesis, which said that God created the heavens and the earth in six days and on the seventh day he rested.

Their week began and ended on the same days as the Babylonian one. But, unlike the Babylonians, who merely rested on the seventh day, the Hebrews made the seventh day their sabbath, a day of prayer and religious ceremonies.

These men carrying the book of Genesis in their luggage back to Jerusalem had mixed feelings about astrology. Its strange cult of star magic was rather popular— too popular to please the rabbis and other leaders, who regarded it as superstitious nonsense and probably evil. That is why they refused to let any of the names of the days of the week be mentioned anywhere in their Bible.

They called the days first day, second day, third day,

fourth day, fifth day, sixth day, and Sabbath. Now the Russians, Greeks, Portuguese, Chinese, and the eastern European nations still use numbers instead of our week-day names.

The early Christians also distrusted astrology. They said it was superstitious. They called it idolatry. For a long while they refused to use the names of the days.

Then who did carry the week-day names around Europe? Not the astrologers, who were selling their expensive secrets only to a few rich people. Yet somebody spread those names.

The week with its planet names was made popular in Europe by a religion imported from ancient Iran. It was Mithraism.

The Mithraists loved astrology. They made it part of their religion. Gladly accepting the whole rigmarole of planet day names and the beliefs about them (to which, however, the Mithraists gave a peculiar slant of their own) they said a prayer each day to the planet-god for whom that day was named.

What was Mithraism?

Mithras was worshiped in Iran (Persia) long before 1400 B.C. He was a god of light. The soldiers believed he helped them to victory.

Because a soldier has to be brave, Mithras was said to give you courage. Also a soldier must be loyal. You cannot fight well if you do not trust the other men fighting on your side. Therefore this soldiers' god was the spirit of truth and the protector of oaths and promises.

In a mountain meadow at sunrise short-bearded Persians, clutching cloaks around them in the chill of the morning, chanted this prayer while they offered sheep's milk and honey on a stone altar:

"To Mithras, lord of wide pastures, we sacrifice. Hear us, O thou the truth-speaker, the eloquent in assembly, the thousand-eared, the myriad-eyed, the exalted, lord of the broad outlook, Mithras the strong, the shapely, the sleepless, the vigilant!"

If you made a promise in his name, and then broke your promise, he would surely catch you—with all those eyes and ears of his.

And it would do you no good to make excuses. The sacred book said,

"Break not your agreement, whether you have made it with the faithless or with the righteous fellow-believer. Mithras stands for both, for the faithless and for the righteous."

You had to keep your promise even if the other fellow was faithless.

Soldiers often were poor. But in Mithras they had a friend.

"The poor man, the needy, he who follows the teaching of righteousness, when he is wronged or deprived of his rights, lifts up his hands and calls to Mithras for help."

Poor soldiers liked this religion which urged a man to stand up for his rights, to fight for his rights if necessary. And Mithras would help him.

The ancient Iranians (Persians) believed in many gods. But three were most important.

The supreme god was Ormazd (also called Mazda), who was the spirit of what is good. With his long white beard and solemn eyes he sat on a throne far away in the remotest part of the sky. Kings prayed to him before going into battle. But he was too far away to be able to hear common people.

But Ormazd had created graceful Mithras, god of light, to live on earth and help people.

The third god was Ahriman, the spirit of evil, the Prince of Darkness. He lived in the shadows under the world.

About 630 B.C. this religion was reformed by the great prophet Zoroaster. He explained that life is a struggle between good and evil. Always the nasty demons with hoofs and spike-pointed tails, who are sent by the Prince of Darkness, are tempting men and women to be gluttonous, sensual, lazy, and dishonest. But Ormazd above

sends a heavenly host of white-winged angels flapping down from the sky to help all faithful people to fight the good fight.

With the teachings of Zoroaster this religion became much stronger. A whole tribe of priests, called the magi, wearing long robes spangled with silver stars, was organized to preach it. And soon it had a chance to spread.

In 539 B.C. the powerful king Cyrus the Great led his Persian army into Babylonia. It was he who set the Hebrews free and sent them home. And Mithraism began its spectacular march to the west.

In Babylonia the magi learned astrology. Unlike the Hebrew rabbis, who had thought it superstitious and probably evil, the Mithraists liked the mysterious star study. They saw in it a method for increasing their power. The magi studied Babylonian incantations of all kinds and tried so hard to work magic that our word *magic* comes from their name.

The mystic idea that the seven planets rule the days of the week suited them just fine. Each day they chanted prayers to that day's planet.

And they began to preach their religion effectively. As the Persian Empire expanded farther westward, they made a great many converts, especially in the royal courts of the kingdoms in what is now Turkey.

In 335 B.C. Alexander the Great became dictator of Greece and went on the warpath. He was twenty-one years old, a handsome athlete. He had curly yellow hair, powerful shoulders, and almost no human feelings at all. Within five years he and his army conquered Asia Minor, Egypt, Babylonia, and Iran.

He was open-minded about all religions, and Mithraism soon spread into his Greek-speaking cities along the Mediterranean coast all the way from northern Asia Minor to Alexandria in Egypt.

The one most important country where Mithraism was never much accepted was Greece itself. And that is why the names of the days of the week even today are still not used in Greece.

Yet in the Mediterranean countries that Alexander had conquered, the magi ran into so much Greek art and

Greek philosophy and Greek religion and even Greek ways of dressing and eating and talking that in these places Mithraism soon became a different sort of religion from the old Zoroastrianism back home in Iran.

In these western places they began to make pretty statues of Mithras, showing him as a youthful and very noble-looking athlete. They modeled him as nearly as they could like Alexander.

And they translated the names of the days into the Greek language.

The story of how this religion first went to Italy is really funny.

One group of men who took up Mithraism with particularly deep devotion was a large organization of pirates. Sailing from their home at Tarsus in what is now southern Turkey, they used to say prayers to the Iranian god of light, asking him to help them in their profitable raids against the richly laden Roman ships. They even took priests with them on their pirate ships.

As Rome gradually became wealthier and more powerful, the Senate sent soldiers several times to put a stop to these raids. But after each fight the Mithraist pirates (made bold by their religion) got back into business.

At last they went into the kidnaping trade, snatching people and selling them into slavery. The pirate ships appeared at the mouth of the Tiber River in Italy. In 68

B.C. they kidnaped some white-robed government officials right on the sunny Appian Way a few miles from the city of Rome.

That was too much. The Roman Senate voted a large sum of money, many soldiers, and unlimited power to their proud but very shrewd general, Pompey. In forty days he captured and sank all the pirate ships near Italy. He then sailed eastward. Roman methods were not gentle. Within a month and a half he exterminated all the raiders he could find, captured their home towns, and burned their docks and their ships.

A few escaped. And many of the pirates' priests managed to slip away. But they knew that if they went home they would have their heads chopped off. So where did they go to hide? To Italy, of all places!

Within a few years they built several small Mithraist chapels in southern Italy.

As the Roman Empire expanded and became more wealthy, more and more magi journeyed to Italy to seek their fortunes.

Later, when Nero's army, after invading Armenia, made peace with the local government there, the king of Armenia took a trip to Italy. This king was short and fat, and he scrubbed his face so hard that it glistened in the sunlight. He believed himself to be the god Mithras born again. He arrived in Rome, bringing two magi with him.

When they explained their religion to Nero, the half-

mad emperor was delighted and had himself initiated into
its mysteries. However, Nero died soon afterward.

During the next hundred years Mithraism became
more and more popular among the Roman soldiers. Then
the emperors had to take it seriously. Commodus (son
of the philosopher, Marcus Aurelius) decided to be initiated into the cult in A.D. 180.

Christianity was spreading then, too, though many of
its believers were being tortured and slaughtered by the
Roman governors. The Egyptian cult of Isis was popular
in Rome, and so was the mystical religion of the Great
Mother. But the most popular of all was Mithraism, especially in the army.

And when an emperor solemnly took up the worship
of this Iranian god of light, many of the government offi-

33

cials and the wealthy families thought it a good idea too.

We can easily understand why emperors liked it.

Mithraism taught that in each country the supreme god, Ormazd, had personally chosen the king or emperor to rule over the people. And Mithras came and stood invisibly beside the ruler, to give him victory over all his enemies. Naturally emperors found this religion useful.

And soldiers felt its attractions. Since the battles, by which the emperor won these victories, were fought by the soldiers, many of them liked Mithraism because it guaranteed their success.

When it had once really started, it spread rapidly.

One legion of the Roman army, composed largely of recruits from the Mithraist provinces in what is now Turkey, carried the mysterious ceremonies of the unconquerable god to the Danube River and built chapels at Vienna.

Many other Roman soldiers formed Mithraist groups. They built underground chapels and carved religious testimonials which recently have been dug up in France, in Germany, in every Roman city and fort in England, across North Africa, and all through the Balkans. By A.D. 250 Mithraism, using the names of the days of the week, was the one strongest religion all the way from the Atlantic Ocean to the border of India.

The story of Mithras himself is so amazing that we must give it a separate chapter.

The Story of Mithras

This is the story his priests told about *deus solis invictus* (the god unconquered of the sun) and how he came to be called that.

In the days before the great kings the supreme god, Ormazd, found it good in his sight to create the race of man. Coming down from heaven, he looked about for a substance with which to make his creation, and his hand lighted upon the clay of the earth. Of common clay the hand of god formed the first man and the first woman. Ormazd with the breath of his nostrils gave them life. And because they were made of mere clay they must suffer. But because they breathed in their lives with the breath of god, they could hope and strive for the highest.

Ormazd set the first man and the first woman upon the ground. He called the man's name Yima. And the man and woman discovered earth and air and water, and they touched and breathed and drank thereof and called them good.

Then Ahriman, the Prince of Darkness, when he saw the man and the woman, was filled with anger and made up his mind to destroy these creatures whom his enemy had made.

First the chief demon sent a chill winter wind to blow upon them. They took shelter in a great cave under a cliff. But still their limbs shook. And their voices cried out to Ormazd, "O Thou who hast made us, do not desert us, for we shiver in the bitterness of the wind! We are about to perish in the cold of the hills!"

Then Ormazd came to them. He carried in his hand a burning torch and showed them the fire.

But at the sight of the leaping flame the man was afraid, and the woman crouched fearfully behind him.

"Be not afraid," the supreme god told them. "For this flame is my gift to you. Therefore let it be always remembered as the most holy possession of man. Let the fire be called sacred forever."

And the man took the fire and built an altar in the cave and laid the fire thereon. Placing his hands together,

36

he bowed reverently before the gift of the god. And he and the woman warmed themselves and were glad.

And Ormazd returned to heaven, having defeated for the time being the evil purposes of Ahriman.

The Birth of Mithras

Far away in the sky the supreme god—calm, dignified, and remote—bethought him then that people were in need of some other noble god closer to earth than he himself would wish to be. So, on his heavenly couch, where in glowing light he sat surrounded by angel musicians and many lesser gods, he raised himself slightly and looked down at the world.

This time he did not use clay. Selecting a large rock which stood beside the river of life in the shade of the sacred tree of wisdom, Ormazd pointed one finger. And the rock began to groan.

Slowly the rock moved and stretched and groaned again. As beneath the hands of a skillful sculptor a new form grows from the living marble, so the blessed rock gave birth to Mithras.

This god of soldiers was, even from the beginning, a fighting man's ideal. Mithras was strong, brave, loyal, and hard—as hard as a stone.

The only people who witnessed his miraculous birth were some shepherds tending their flocks on a hillside

37

nearby. At first they were afraid and concealed themselves in a cave, daring only to peer out cautiously.

As they watched the god emerge from the rocky mass, he was wearing a Phrygian cap and was armed already with a knife. The leaves murmured musically, and the shadows of that place were lighted by the heavenly glow that radiated around him.

First he bathed in the river of life, and the waters purified him.

Then, finding himself naked and feeling the cold blast of the wind, he entered among the branches of the tree of wisdom. With his knife he cut off the sacred fruit and ate thereof and was satisfied. With his knife he cut off leaves and with them made his first clothing.

At last the shepherds came out of hiding. Approaching the divine youth, they knelt before him and worshiped. Then they offered him the first fruits of their flocks and of their fields, pledging themselves and their children forever to dedicate to Mithras the best of whatever they had. They adorned the god with a shepherd's leggings and woolen tunic, and placed on his left shoulder a shepherd's cloak, which flapped gaily in the breeze.

And Mithras, the exalted one, the truth-speaker, the eloquent in assembly, lifted up his voice and instructed the shepherds, saying, "Now I will teach you how to pray. First you are to make your devotions to Ormazd, god of light and goodness, for it was he who sent me to be among you, and this is his light which I bring with me. Next you are to speak your daily conjuration to Ahriman, Prince of Darkness, the spirit of evil, asking him not to lead you into temptation. And, thirdly, you are to incline your heads humbly to Time eternal, who created both Ormazd and Ahriman, for Time brings both good and evil.

"And now I will teach you the wisdom of life. Although Time has created both good and evil, it has made good unconquerable, but it has not made evil unconquerable. Therefore I enlist you as my first recruits to stand on my side, the side of light, and to fight the good fight in the sacred struggle against evil. To the brave man comes victory, and to the active man success. He who is loyal and follows righteousness, let him call upon me when he is in need, for to the faithful I am all ears and to the devout I am all eyes. Though the call come in the darkest hour, I am ever watchful. When the need arises, I am wakeful."

With a sudden clatter of hoofs the four fierce horses of the sun galloped down the hillside to the shore of the river of life, where Mithras stood. Behind them the majestic sun god in his blazing chariot pulled hard on the reins, till the beasts reared up, neighing. Angrily the sun god leaped to earth, his eyes wide with menace, and strode forward, swinging his sword.

Looking scornfully at Mithras, he demanded, "Who is

this newcomer who brings light with him to the earth? Be off, I warn you! For none shall shed light here but I. Am I not sole ruler of the sun chariot and lord of light? I am known by many names, for all nations honor me. I am Hvar of the Iranians, Shamash of the Babylonians, Helios and Apollo of the Greeks. I will not share my honors. Therefore be gone!"

But Mithras answered, "Now I call Ormazd to witness, who made us both: I will neither flee nor hide. For I have come to earth to fight the good fight, helping men against the forces of evil. Therefore I stand firm, shedding my light in dark corners wherever I go. And he who would prevent me shall feel the strength of my hands."

"Enough! Blasphemer!" cried the mighty sun god furiously. "You take the name of the lord our god in vain. Now stand ready to perish!" Raising his flame-bright sword, he rushed at Mithras.

But the rock-born young god seized the wrist of Helios, wrenched the sword from him, threw it down in one direction and hurled the flaming god to earth in the other direction.

Panting, Helios rose from the trodden ground. "Be not overbold," he warned. "No one has ever fought with me and come off unconquered." And he rushed at Mithras again.

All day they fought. Twice Mithras was driven from the field, but each time he returned. The third time he was thrown against the rocky cliff from whence he had been born. As he felt the stony surface under his fingers, new courage and new strength flowed into him. With one final lunge he seized the sun god, threw him violently to earth, and with his knife stepped forward to cut off his head.

But Helios, seeing himself at last defeated, rose on one knee and begged to be spared. "For if I go, who shall drive the four-horsed chariot of the sun each day across the heavens to make glad the hearts of men? I now see that you really are the son of Ormazd, for no one else could have withstood me. And when you said that he had sent you to fight the good fight, helping men against the forces of evil, you spoke truth."

Mithras agreed to spare him, and added, "You shall be henceforth the undisputed ruler of the sun chariot and its horses. And in witness of your sovereign power I now place upon your head the radiant crown." And Mithras placed on the head of the kneeling sun god the crown of kingship, with rays symbolizing the light of the sun, such as kings have worn ever since.

Then Helios rose, and the two gods shook hands, pledging themselves to be brothers and allies forever. And Helios said to him, "You are the only one who has fought even with the sun and has not been conquered. Therefore you shall be known from this day forward forever as the unconquered of the sun."

Then Phosphoros, the gods' messenger, flew out of the sky to witness their pact of friendship. Stepping lightly onto the earth, he folded his bright wings of many colors and approached the two gods with benediction. And he placed a couch for them to rest on, and a table with fine foods that they might eat. And Mithras and Helios reclined on the couch together and broke bread and ate, and they drank wine together, after pouring a libation to the powers of heaven and of hell.

And when they had eaten together the meal of brother-hood, they rose up and mounted into the sun chariot, Mithras and Helios. Phosphoros flew beside them, blowing a horn, and the whole assemblage of the gods watched and approved as the brother gods rode in the sun chariot across the ocean. Poseidon, the bull-horned god of the sea, signaled his approval, while beside him his wife Amphitrite waved a message of good will.

In his travels over the earth Mithras made many friends. The fiery lion crouched before him. The serpent came from the earth and was tamed by him. But Mithras' favorite friend and most faithful companion was the quick and clever dog.

Mithras spoke with the four seasons and with the four winds, and traveled with each of them in turn. And he spoke with the twelve constellations of the zodiac and with the seven planets. And all the stars of heaven honored this god of light, sworn brother of the sun.

Now, at this time the supreme god, Ormazd, created a great bull. The horns of this bull were of the whitest ivory, its shoulders were like the mountains for strength, and its roar was like the thunder.

When Mithras saw the bull, he longed to capture it and to tame it as a friend. Calling his sharp-nosed dog to go with him, he set out on the chase. Mithras pursued the bull over mountains and through valleys, across rivers and through storms. And always the bull escaped him.

But one day at last he came upon the wild beast grazing in a mountain meadow. This time when the great bull saw Mithras approaching, it wheeled about, turning its face toward him, and lowered its head. Its sharp front hoofs scraped the ground, and the breath from its nostrils blew up the dust.

As the bull charged, Mithras seized its horns, vaulted over its head, and landed on its back.

The bull reared up and tried to jab him, but he held onto the horns. The bull jumped and bucked, but Mithras held on.

Then the bull galloped away. For forty days they fled furiously over mountains, through valleys, across rocky deserts. Sometimes Mithras rode, sometimes he was thrown off and dragged. But always he held on.

At last they came back to the same mountain meadow, Mithras riding triumphantly on the exhausted bull. As it reached the center of the meadow it collapsed, defeated.

Then the young god bethought him how he might take the tamed bull home. It was too much worn out to walk. Seizing it by the hind legs, which he pulled over his shoulders, he carried the animal on his back.

When they came to the seashore he found a shepherd's cabin, and they went inside. Here he discovered a sheep, freshly killed. And he cooked it and ate it and laid himself down to rest during the night.

But suddenly in the dark hours they were wakened by angry shouting. Looking out the doorway of the gabled hut, Mithras saw it surrounded by a multitude of demons, yelling and waving three-pointed spears.

Quieting their noise by a gesture, he demanded, "Who are you that disturb the sleep of peaceful travelers in the night, and what do you want? If you have come here seeking that which is rightfully mine, you shall go back empty-handed. For I am Mithras, the unconquered of the sun."

One of the demons shouted, "We are servants of Ahriman, the Prince of Darkness. We know you well, Mithras, god of light, and we are not your friends, nor are we friendly to anyone who is your companion. We have come to take the bull, for it is no ordinary bull but contains within it the seeds of the whole creation of the bread of man. Therefore we have orders from our prince that you must give the animal into our hands, and we shall slay it and destroy the seed."

And they came forward to attack the cabin, hooting and waving torches.

Mithras looked about for a weapon. His eye lighting on the bones of the sheep which he had eaten, he took up the largest bone, rushed out to meet the demons, and killed many of them, breaking their heads with the bone.

But the demons set fire to the building. Feeling the heat of the raging flames, the bull, in terror for its life, rushed forth into the hands of those who would undo it.

Mithras, laying about him mightily with the sheep's bone, beat off the demons who had seized the bull. Leading the animal down to the edge of the water, he got it into a ship which was there, and together they set sail across the sea and came to the other side just at daybreak.

And after many other troubles he at last brought the bull home to his cave, where they lived peacefully together for three years.

But one sad day the croaking raven, messenger of the sun god, came flying over the hills. (And in later years in the underground chapels two priests used to chant the litany of their meeting. One priest wore a head mask of a raven. The other wore the Phrygian cap of Mithras.)

"I come for Mithras, the unconquered of the sun."

"Say on, O Raven. No one calls to me unheard."

"You are not he whom I seek, for the one I seek has a companion who is a great black bull."

"I begin to fear your message. Yet tell it with courage, for I have a companion who is a great black bull."

"Then I bring you sorrowful news. You are to have that companion no longer."

"Your news is as dark as your wings, O raven. How am I to lose my companion?"

"With your own hands you are to spill on the earth all the might of that bull."

46

"*Surely you speak falsely, for I would not kill my friend.*"

"Surely I speak truth, for you shall sink your knife into his flank."

"*How can this be? For he who loves righteousness is ever loyal to his companions.*"

"These are the orders of the sun god, your sworn brother."

"*How keenly I remember my joy when I first looked upon the bull!*"

"Sometimes for a higher reason we must sacrifice that which is dearest to us."

"*And what is the higher reason for this most bitter sacrifice?*"

"The blood of the sacred bull must flow for the good of all mankind."

Mithras concluded simply, "This is a sad day for me."

Knowing that he must unquestionably obey orders, he put aside his grief and went to seek the bull in its usual pasture. But when he arrived, his friend was not there. Mithras looked on all sides, but at the sound of the voice of the raven, the powerful beast had fled.

Whistling to his dog, the sorrowful young god began the search. Quickly the sharp-nosed dog picked up the fresh scent, and together they set out in pursuit of the bull.

47

In another valley they caught sight of it, and for the last time Mithras looked with admiration at the ivory-white horns and mountainous shoulders. But Mithras was born of a rock and knew how to harden his heart when duty commanded.

Swiftly he ran down across the valley and seized his former companion as the bull was about to enter a sheltering cave.

Placing one foot on one of its rear hoofs to make it stumble, he kneeled on its back, took hold of it by the nostrils with his left hand, and with his right hand sank his knife into its flank. The great god-created beast roared like thunder for the last time.

The dog leaped forward to assist at the kill. And the other friends of Mithras gathered to witness his noble sacrifice. The lion crouched before him. The snake rose up, writhing, from the earth. The four winds blew, and the four seasons called out with a loud cry.

Then all these companions witnessed the greatest miracle that had ever occurred. For this was no ordinary bull but contained within it the seeds of the whole creation of the bread of man.

From the body of the dying god-created beast all the grasses were born, from the parts of the body all the healthful plants that men may eat. Out of the rich white marrow of its spine came wheat, which gives bread. Issuing from the end of its tail, the first ears of wheat

48

sprang forth into the sunlight. And these green growing things spread themselves out across the wide valley and into the next valley and over the whole world. Every fertile field received its covering of verdure, every meadow its life-giving green mantle.

And from the rich blood, which flowed copiously from the wound, grape vines sprang up and clusters of grapes, that men might drink of the fruit of the vine and make their hearts glad with the wine thereof.

The powers of heaven took notice of the miracle. The moon goddess, who was great Mah of the Iranians, noble Sin of the Babylonians, lovely Selene of the Greeks, gathered up the remains of the bull. Spreading these in different parts of the world, she produced all the species of useful animals: the horse, the cow, the pig, the camel, the elephant, and the other friends of man. The seed of the sacred bull produced all those that give of their work, their milk, or their flesh to enrich the lives of men.

What was left of the bull was its noble soul, which, protected by the dog, was lifted slowly up to heaven. Angels blowing golden horns came to receive it. And they welcomed it into the celestial kingdom, where it took form as a new archangel, called (in Latin) Silvanus. Thenceforth this archangel was the heavenly guardian of all good flocks.

Thus Mithras by his heroic sacrifice became the creator of the kind and helpful living things. He brought into the world all animals and plants that do us good. From the death which he had caused was born a new and richer life.

With joy and thanksgiving people received these gifts. The children and grandchildren of the man and woman whom Ormazd had created gathered the fruits of the field, the wheat and the grapes. They herded together the various kinds of useful animals. Dedicating the best of each flock to the truth-speaker, the young god of light, they made sacrifices on their altars, where the sacred fire burned perpetually, and gave thanks to their benefactor.

The shepherds who had witnessed the birth of Mithras from the rock had told the people thereof and had instructed them in the mysteries of the god's teachings and of man's fellowship with Mithras.

Remembering the feast of brotherhood between the mighty sun god and young Mithras the unconquered of the sun, the people, sitting together, broke bread and ate. Reverently they poured libations and drank of the sacred wine. And together they banqueted on the good flesh of the dedicated beasts. With handclasps the men swore loyalty to one another. With oaths they promised to live in righteousness and in truth and always to call Mithras to aid them in their fights against their enemies. And they rose from the feast feeling strong and whole at heart and went their ways in brotherhood.

When the Prince of Darkness saw them, he realized that his purpose had been defeated. His chill winter wind, which he had sent against them long ago, had not destroyed them. Anger filled him, and he again determined to rid the earth of them.

When they had planted their crops and had put their herds out to pasture, Ahriman sent a great drought, which desolated the countryside. Day after day the sun shone, but never a cloud appeared, not any drop of rain. At night Ahriman withheld the dew from the withering fields. And the flocks died, the crops burned brown, and men's throats were parched with the dryness.

"Come," said one of the shepherds, "let us call to Mithras, for he is our defender." Raising an altar in a meadow at the foot of a great cliff, the people laid twigs and logs on it and brought the sacred fire. When the flames leaped upward, the men prayed with sad voices. Prostrating themselves on the hard, cracked soil, they wept for their defender.

And the young god heard them and responded to their call. Lightly he sped to them across the meadow, his cloak blowing gaily in the wind. On his shoulder he bore a bow and a quiver of arrows.

When he stood before them, the people rushed to the shapely god and knelt about him. Pointing to their dry throats, they implored him to find water to ease their suffering.

Thoughtfully Mithras surveyed the great cliff. Then he fitted an arrow to his bow. With a loud voice he called out, "O Ormazd, my heavenly father, hear my prayer and save these people!"

Mithras let fly the swift arrow against the cliff. Where the arrow struck, the rock parted with a thunderous crack. And a great spout of water gushed forth. Fresh

52

water streamed from the face of the cliff. It ran down through the meadow in a rushing river.

Joyfully the people kneeled beside the hurrying water, dipped in their hands, and carried it to their mouths. And with a great shout they gave thanks to Mithras.

Then they brought their flocks that they, too, might

drink. And, digging channels, the men conveyed the life-giving fluid through their fields.

So were they saved, by the grace of Mithras.

And they lived in peace for many years.

But Ahriman called his demons together and made plans once more to destroy them.

On a still summer day the rock-born god, the truth-speaker, shapely Mithras, appeared secretly at the door of the house of a shepherd, an old man bowed down with the weight of years. The young god said to him, "Arise, old man, and do as I am about to instruct you."

The old man placed his hands together and gave thanks for the favor being shown to him.

Mithras told him, "You will take tools and go into the forest with your servants and cut wood. And with this wood you are to build an ark, even here on the hillside in front of your house. And the people will come and laugh at you, asking, 'Old man, are you out of your wits, to build a boat on dry land, far from any water?' You shall not heed them but shall build your ark, for your god loves an active man, and Mithras loves an obedient man who is not idle. And in the autumn season, as soon as the crops are harvested, you shall gather your grain into the ark and all the animals, two by two, and go aboard with your family. This do, and you shall live to be grateful."

So the old man built the ark on the hillside in front of his house. And the people laughed and mocked at him, saying, "He builds a boat on dry land!" But he did not heed them. And at the end of the harvest season, when he had stowed the grain and all the kinds of animals on board, he went up into the ark, he and his family.

And a great rain descended on the earth. All the streams became rivers, the swollen rivers overflowed their banks, and the waves of the sea invaded the dry land. Like an angry army the waves came, and beat open every door.

The people cried out in terror. Their fields were destroyed, their cattle drowned. They saw their houses washed away. As they themselves swam in the flood, they heard the harsh laughter of Ahriman, the Prince of Darkness, who had sent the abundant waters for the destruction of men. "God is my enemy," said Ahriman, "and either his children, his playthings made of clay, shall perish utterly, or I shall, in the end."

But the ark floated on the billows. For many days the old shepherd and his family rocked to and fro and were too terrified to look out.

But at last the tempest subsided. They opened a window, and the wind and rain beat their faces yet a little while and then ceased. A few days later the ark came to rest on a high point of land.

When the ocean had gone back to its beaches, and the rivers and streams to their winding courses, the sun shone and the muddy fields steamed under its warmth. At last

the old shepherd and his family led out their animals. All together the men bowed their knees, reverently giving thanks to the unconquered of the sun, who had delivered them. Then they brought forth the seeds of the harvest, and the sons of the family planted crops, for Mithras had told them that man does not live the good life by idleness.

The days of Mithras upon the world were coming to an end. By his heroic deeds which he had accomplished, the attempts of his enemy to destroy mankind had been defeated.

Then for the last time the young god, the truth-speaker, the ever-watchful, the unconquered of the sun, came to give his benediction to the family of man. As they knelt before him beside the ark, birds flew overhead, the sunlight sparkled on the earth, and little brooks ran cheerfully between the warm fields.

Mithras said to them, "Hear my last words to you, and store up my instructions in your hearts. I have taught you how to pray and have revealed to you the wisdom of life. When you die in the flesh, your souls will come to me. I shall meet you on the bridge into heaven. And those among you who shall have lived in righteousness and in truth, keeping faith with one another and with the laws of Mithras, I shall welcome with glad smiles. Them shall I pass along the bridge to their peace in eternal glory near the heavenly hosts of Ormazd, our creator. But those who shall have been cowards on earth, or unfaithful, yielding to the temptations of Ahriman, Prince of Darkness, to wallow in gluttony, idleness, and deceit, them shall I reject. To sinners my heart is of stone. I shall bar the bridge of heaven against them and shall cast them down. And the demons of Ahriman shall take them into hell, where the flames shall lick them, and they shall live to the end of the world in all manner of torments.

"Therefore, remember the law and live cleanly.

"Now I am about to leave you for a little while. But, even though in heaven, I shall always be with you in spirit. Your calls will always be answered. My strength will be with you when you invoke me in aid against your enemies. My right arm will hold you from temptation if you pray to me in your hour of need.

"And at the time of the end of the world, I shall return. You shall be forewarned when you see the great disasters which Ahriman will send upon you then in his last battle against the forces of righteousness. For in those days wars will spread over the whole world, and new diseases, and burning lights—false suns created by Ahriman, raining destruction from the sky. False prophets shall shout from the house tops, leading great masses of men in hatred against one another. Fools and idiots shall jabber in the streets, and wise men die in dark corners. Thus shall you know that the end has come.

"Then a marvelous bull will appear on earth, in every way like the original one which I sacrificed for your sakes. Then you shall hear my call, a great call, resounding in every ear. At my call, all the dead shall arise from their graves and walk in flesh once more. The walking dead, come back to life, shall fill every street, every country road and path. All shall be counted—every one—and none shall be missing. On that day I shall assemble the

58

multitudes of the nations, and I shall divide the good from the evil.

"As my final sacrifice I shall once more kill the bull. I shall mix its grease with the sacred wine and give this drink to all the good people, whom it will make perfect and immortal. Then they shall have life eternal on this earth.

"But Ormazd, god of light, will send from heaven a great fire that will burn up stables and barns and all the signs of labor by the hands of man. And in his final fire the doers of evil—the liars, the idle, the unfaithful—shall perish utterly. Their very names will be forgotten, and no one will speak of them again.

"In that fire proud Ahriman, Prince of Darkness, and all his demons shall perish with the damned whom they have tormented. For good shall triumph on that day. And thenceforth the universe shall be perfect and eternal."

While he was speaking these last words of consolation, the mighty sun god came down to him, even to the meadow where Mithras stood. Helios came riding in the sun chariot. Mithras then mounted into the flaming chariot and waved farewell to his friends whom he was leaving behind on earth. And the four great horses, responding to the call of the sun god, carried the chariot away into heaven.

How the Week Went
Round the World

OBVIOUSLY the Mithraists, when passing through Babylon, had picked up some of the same stories that the Hebrews, while in Babylon, had used in putting together the book of Genesis. But always the Mithraists gave each story their own slant.

In Babylon, also, the Mithraists had picked up their love of astrology (which the Hebrews had wisely rejected).

An ancient Roman gravestone, after giving the dead man's name, tells what he was: "Of Mithras the invincible of the sun, priest, and student of astrology."

Many Mithraist priests became students of astrology.

If you visited a Mithraist chapel, you would see the worship of the planets, for whom our days of the week were named. Going in from the street, you entered a small lobby decorated with a few columns. If you could open the door at the back of the lobby (but you were not allowed to open it unless you had been initiated), you went down into the crypt. Mithraist chapels were all built like caves (because caves were considered holy).

In the darkness you would see candles burning and perhaps hear a bell announcing that the ceremony was about to begin. Ahead of you, at the far end of the vault, a flickering red and yellow fire burned on an altar.

When your eyes became accustomed to the dim light, you would see that the chapel was small, scarcely big enough for a hundred people. Under the curved ceiling like a cave's, you would see a central corridor about thirty-three feet long and eight feet wide, going straight from you to the altar, with a long raised platform on each side about four feet wide, running the whole length of the corridor. On these two platforms the worshipers—all men—would be assembling. Some knelt, saying their prayers. Others lay face down.

The dampness, the dark, the murmur of many voices, and the heavy smell of incense might make you feel odd.

At the most dramatic moment of the ceremony, a priest would pull aside the deep blue velvet curtain behind the altar, revealing the sculptured relief of Mithras slaying the bull. There stood the young god, all in natural colors, in his shepherd's costume and Phrygian cap, his cloak blowing gaily in the breeze. One knee was on the animal's back, his knife in its side, the blood pouring forth painted bright red.

In the mosaic design on the walls seven stations were marked, one for each planet. Each day a priest stood at the station of that day's planet, where the mosaic showed a portrait of the god of that planet, and chanted the prayers for that day.

So that astrology would be more popular, the Mithraists had made each planet-god almost human. The planet-god who ruled over you (because you were born on his day) felt pleased when you were good. And when you did anything wrong, he (or she) became angry. Then you had to try to make friends with him again by giving gifts to the chapel and by saying special prayers.

After you died, your soul continued to be fully conscious and knew just what was happening. Escorted by angels and pursued by demons, it went up toward heaven. If you had been good enough, so that Mithras would permit you to pass along the bridge of heaven, you found you had seven flights of stairs to climb. On the seven landings some amazing things happened.

First you passed the moon, and, as you did so, the moon goddess took away your appetite for food. At the top of the next stairway you came to Mercury, with whom you left all your desire for money and possessions. When you passed Venus you left your desire for love. When you passed the sun, you left your brain power. (You were not going to need *that* in the Mithraists' heaven!)

When you passed Mars, Jupiter, and Saturn, you left your quarrelsomeness, your ambitions, and your laziness. So at heaven's gate you had nothing left. You were perfect. At least, that was their idea of how to be perfect.

(Nowadays Moslems still talk of going up to the "seventh heaven," where a soul will have nothing left except bliss.)

Believing the planets to be so important, the Mithraists naturally took the seven-day week entirely for granted.

They were the ones who spread the week, for it was not official in the Roman Empire. The Roman calendar consisted of the same months as we have now (including a 29th of February on leap years). And it had official holidays on certain days of each month. The ides was the thirteenth of the month (the fifteenth of some months). The nones came eight days before the ides. And so on. These were days for celebrations. In small towns the market days were usually arranged to occur every eighth day (a different day in different towns). These holidays broke up the months into something like

63

irregular weeks. But they occurred on all different days of the seven-day astrologers' week.

This was the calendar of the official state religion. It had holidays in honor of Jupiter, Juno, Pluto, Mars, Venus, and their companions. As time passed, these holidays became like Fourth of July and Labor Day, without any genuine religious feelings. And of course this state religion did not use the seven-day week.

In the later days of the empire (from A.D. 200 to A.D. 300) two other religions did have real meaning and became extremely popular in Rome: the cult of Isis and the cult of Cybele, the Great Mother. These cults, too, had many big celebrations on certain days of certain months (as our Christmas comes on December 25 no matter what day of the week it may be). Neither of them used the week.

The seven-day week was used by the Christians and Jews, but at that time most of them refused to say the names of the days.

Consequently, if it had not been for the Mithraists we would not have our names for the days now.

Actually Mithraism was so widespread and its influences were so strong in the Roman Empire that by A.D. 250 our week was commonly known all over the Roman Empire—in England, France, western Germany, Austria, Italy, the Balkans, and in North Africa, Egypt, Palestine, and in what is now Turkey.

The Translation of the Week

When the Mithraists first came to Italy and learned about the Roman gods, they tried to believe that these were really their own gods with different names. Who was Jupiter? Oh, that must be another name for Ormazd. Who was Venus? That must be another name for Anahita (their goddess of the growing crops).

In doing this they made some strange mixtures. In reading the story of Mithras you may have been surprised to learn that Poseidon had bull's horns. In studying Greek mythology you never heard that! Yet Mithraist sculpture shows him with horns. You have noticed, too, how they changed the story of Noah and the Flood.

The Mithraists always translated other people's gods into their religion. They made over the Roman shepherds' god Silvanus into their own archangel of the herds. This habit explains how the names of the days of the week were translated into the old language of Germany, from which those names came into English.

Mithraist Roman soldiers in forts all along the Rhine River met and talked day after day with the Teutons who lived there. It was those soldiers and those local inhabitants together who translated the days. The cult of Mithras was particularly strong on the Rhine, where it lasted about a hundred and sixty years (A.D. 90 to A.D. 250).

We can imagine the Roman soldiers in a fort, wearing

65

helmets and short swords, courting the local women or buying vegetables from them. (Most Roman soldiers were vegetarians.) Or they would be talking with Teuton prisoners after a battle. Often, too, they talked with tough, strong young Teuton men who joined the Roman army as new recruits.

Those Teutons were evidently puzzled at first by the seven-day week with its days named after gods or planets. The first two—called "the day of the sun" and "the day of the moon"—were easy to understand. But the others? They were named for Mars, Mercury, Jupiter, Venus, and Saturn. Who were those?

The Roman soldiers explained. "They're not gods exactly. They are gods, but they are really the planets."

To the Teutons this sounded like nonsense. Can you blame them? And they had never heard of planets.

The Mithraists, meanwhile, were trying to understand the Teutons. That, also, was difficult.

The Mithraist soldiers asked, "What do you call our gods in your language?" They learned that the principal Teutonic gods (at that time) were the sun, the moon, Tiu, Woden, Thor, and Frigg. Also, there were others: Loki, Freya, and so on.

The Mithraists showed no respect for this foreign religion. Their idea was to prove that each of these was really one of their own gods in disguise. Only they had trouble deciding which was which.

66

The Teutons and the Roman soldiers talked and argued about this for a long time. And naturally the Romans' understanding of the Teutonic gods at first was different from what they decided later on, after they had talked over the problem for a hundred years. For instance, at first they thought the Teutonic god Tiu was Hercules. Later they figured Tiu must be Mars. They never did find out who he really was.

In the end the soldiers and the Teutons together decided that Thor and Jupiter were somewhat alike. These both hurled the thunderbolts. Tiu was god of war, like Mars. Frigg might—perhaps—be Venus. (We know she was not. But those soldiers were certainly not scholars, and they made mistakes.) They had a hard time with Woden but concluded he must be Mercury. (That was a wild guess!) They never did find any Teutonic god like Saturn.

Using these gods' names, they translated the days of the week into the Teutonic language. The following chapters will explain the names of the days one by one. Also, those chapters will tell the grand old stories of the northern gods.

Later several groups of the Teutons went to England, taking with them the Teutonic names of the days. Their dialect of that old language is called Anglo-Saxon. In England it slowly developed into English. Names like *Wodnesdag* changed little by little through the many centuries, till they became as we now say them. That one became *Wednesday*.

Other dialects of that old Teutonic language eventually became modern German, Dutch, Danish, Swedish, Norwegian, and Icelandic. In these languages the days of the week have the same names that we use—with a few exceptions.

Four religions—the cults of Mithras, Cybele, Isis, and Christ—became intense rivals in the Roman Empire.

The cult of Isis had more than fifty temples in the city of Rome. It was the favorite religion of Pompeii at the time when that city was buried by the volcano (A.D. 79). Until A.D. 312 the cult prospered. So did the cult of Cybele, which was popular with women.

Mithraism also rode high. From A.D. 180 to A.D. 312 all the Roman emperors were Mithraists. (As chiefs of the army, they had to be.)

Christianity was becoming strong in Greece, Egypt, North Africa—the places where Mithraism was weak. But the Christians were regarded as dangerous. They were said to be disobedient revolutionists. Once in a while a Roman governor, becoming alarmed by their strength and their disobedience, would take away their property, put them in prison, torture them, feed them to lions in big colosseums while crowds watched and cheered.

Naturally the Christians thought Mithraism was particularly bad, and tried hard to convert people away from it.

In the New Testament three magi or wise men, we are told, came to worship the infant Jesus in his manger. They brought expensive gifts: gold, frankincense, and myrrh. Many people have wondered who these three men were and how they happened to be so rich. In the Middle Ages people assumed that because they were rich they were kings.

69

But they were not kings.

The text was written in Greek, and the word used there is *magoi*. Students of Mithraism now point out that that was what the Mithraist priests were called in that part of the world (though not in Europe). And as the magi said they could work magic, and charged high prices to do it, they sometimes became rich.

In case any early Christians had doubts as to whether their religion was better than Mithraism, the Gospel according to Saint Matthew says clearly that at least three of the Mithraist magi had bowed down and worshiped Christ. The moral of the story was that therefore the other Mithraists ought to do the same.

Meanwhile Mithraism made several mistakes. One was

that it accepted men only. Its chapels excluded women.

Often a temple to Cybele, the Great Mother, was built next door. While the men were praying to Mithras down in the crypt, their mothers, their aunts, and their wives were having a nice service (actually a much pleasanter service) in the rather gorgeous temple of Cybele.

The cult of Isis was for both men and women.

And Christianity was for everyone, slaves included— though in the churches in those days the women had to sit at one side and keep quiet.

Another weakness of Mithraism was that many men joined it merely because they wanted to be seen going to the right chapel, where their emperor and most of the soldiers went. In other words, many men became Mithraists without caring much about it.

But to become a Christian was dangerous. A person did not risk going to a church unless he cared a great deal about the faith.

Consequently in the year A.D. 300, although there were more Mithraists than Christians, actually the Christians were stronger.

Then suddenly they broke free.

In A.D. 312 the chief of the Roman troops in Britain and Gaul became a Christian. His name was Constantine. Within the following year he got control of most of the European part of the Roman Empire.

Constantine restored the property taken recently from

Christians, stopped the persecution of them in his part of the Empire, and proclaimed equal rights for all religions —including Christianity.

Christians came out of hiding all over Italy and Gaul. And thousands of Mithraists, who had never cared much about religion, lost interest in its chapels.

Constantine gradually got control of North Africa and Greece. At last he became emperor of the whole Roman Empire. He went east and founded the city of Constantinople.

Also he called together a big meeting of Christian bishops to discuss matters of doctrine and to decide what they were going to do, now that for them everything was changed. Rapidly Christianity became the official religion of the government.

The result was amazing.

When the emperor and the high officials had become Christians, the priests converted many men from Mithraism. As soon as the Christians dared, crowds of them stormed into the Mithraist chapels and destroyed them. This was fairly easy to do, as the chapels were underground. If you threw the statues in the river, knocked down the door and the upper part of the stairway, and tossed a little mud on the place, the chapel simply disappeared.

Often there were fights. In Alexandria an angry mob killed the Christian bishop. But in the end the Christians won. In a town in western Germany, for example, they put the Mithraist priest in chains, laid him in his chapel, and buried the whole thing. (He has recently been dug up, chains and all.)

All Mithraist books were seized. Some were burned. Others, written on parchment, were carefully stored away in Christian churches. When the priests and the monks had time, they took sharp knives, sliced off the old writing, and copied down Christian prayers or saints' lives instead. (These sliced-down books are called palimpsests. When you look at old manuscripts in a museum you often can see very faintly the traces of pagan writing under the Christian paragraphs. Sometimes they did not slice deep enough, and nowadays after the newer writing has been carefully photographed, it can be removed by chemicals, which reveal the older writing underneath.)

The newly freed Christians attacked the temples of Jupiter and Venus as soon as they dared, and the temples of Isis and Cybele, of course. In many places, however, the people loved these cults so dearly that the wiser Christian leaders decided not to destroy those religions entirely but to adopt what was best in them. The cult of Isis was particularly noble and worthy of respect. Some of the best bits of Christian ritual and belief come from it.

But the one cult the Christians hated most was Mithraism—which, by the bye, was not a very good religion, as it was full of superstitions and cruelty. It had taught

73

people to harden their hearts. Plenty of people at last hardened their hearts against Mithraism.

By the year A.D. 500 it had disappeared so completely that it was to be found only among ignorant peasants in three or four isolated valleys in the eastern Alps Mountains. Then it vanished even from there.

Vanished?

Yet we still have the names of the days of the week.

Also we still find among us in America and in Europe some old Mithraist customs, such as the Saturday night bath, and many old Mithraist beliefs in luck, in devils, in the evil eye, in magic spells and incantations, and in astrology.

Mithraists used to say, for instance, that Ahriman, the Prince of Darkness, got loose at midnight. Then he roamed about, looking for mischief. If he found a person out of doors in those gloomy hours he would pounce on him, beat him, make him lame or blind or crazy, and go off chuckling. At the first cockcrow Ahriman fled back to his home in hell. Plenty of uneducated people still are afraid of the dark between the "witching hour" (midnight) and the first cockcrow.

The way to protect yourself from the devil was to make magic signs with your finger, say magic words, light a candle, and ring a bell. For centuries afterward people continued to do all this.

Although the hammers of the angry early Christians

74

could destroy buildings, no hammers can break a custom if people believe in it.

After the sudden collapse of Mithraism the people who still believed in astrology had to try to separate themselves from the no longer respectable religion as best they could. Some astrologers fled to Egypt. When they returned they quietly spread the false idea that astrology was from Egypt and that it had nothing to do with Mithraism.

And they more or less secretly kept on teaching that the seven planets, ruling the days of the week, could decide what sort of person you would be. Their beliefs eventually brought some curious words into English:

If you were born on Sunday (under the influence of the sun), you had a *sunny* disposition, wanting to be cheerful.

If you were influenced by the moon (if you were a Monday child), you were *moon-struck*. You would go *mooning* about the house, wanting to dream. And if Luna (the moon) got hold of your wits, you became a *lunatic*.

If you were influenced by the planet Mars, you had a *martial* temperament, wanting to fight.

If you were influenced by Mercury, you were *mercurial*, often wanting to change.

If you were influenced by Jupiter (in Latin his day was *dies Jovis*), you were *jovial*, wanting to laugh and have a good time with people.

75

If you were born on Friday (in Latin *dies Veneris*), you would be of a *venerean* disposition, wanting to make love. This word was for a while considered naughty at the time when the Puritans ruled England. You were not supposed to say it. Now we don't consider it naughty. But, as it has not been used for the last three centuries, no one will know what you are talking about.

If you were a Saturday's child, influenced by Saturn, you would be *saturnine*, which means gloomy. And, as Saturday ever since about 2400 B.C. in ancient Babylon was considered an unlucky day, people still say, "Saturday's child must work for a living."

Mithraism spread these ideas in Europe so strongly that sixteen centuries have not rubbed them all out.

Also, hundreds and hundreds of Mithraist statues and a large number of chapels have recently been dug up. In a museum in London I saw a relief of Mithras slaying the bull, which had been found deep in a muddy bank of the Thames. In the Vatican Museum at Rome I saw three of those familiar statues of Mithras. (The enemy god has come to rest.)

But the Mithraists did not believe in beauty. They thought most artists were cowards. Fine works of art seemed to them sissified. Nowadays critics agree that Mithraist statues—though often made by expert stone-cutters—are not very good. You might look at some and see what you think.

76

They were not intended to be beautiful works of art.
They were made for a purpose: to help dull-minded soldiers, who had not been given much education, to have
a mystical experience. The priests worked up an impres-
sive ritual in which, after much singing and praying, a
curtain was drawn aside and the men were allowed to
"see their god face to face." Then the images looked almost alive, for they seemed to move a little, lighted by
flickering torches.

Always they show the god in the same position, with
one knee on the bull's back. Sometimes two figures are

beside him in very casual positions, each standing on one foot. These are two extra representations of Mithras himself, one holding up a torch, the other holding a torch down. Their meaning was complicated. (Mithraists loved to make things complicated.) They symbolized Mithras as god of dawn and as god of evening. They also symbolized several other ideas, including Mithras pointing the torch upward to light good souls on their way to heaven, and downward to send bad souls to hell. The casualness of the poses indicated that Mithras did not care. The Roman soldiers' ideal was a person who had no feelings.

What is your opinion of them?

The week went to India after the conquests of Alexander the Great. His armies passed through Palestine, Babylonia, Iran, and entered the edge of India. He opened trade routes connecting those countries. The Indian sages were eager to learn. They got the week from Babylonia and translated the planet names of the days into Sanskrit. A large number of astrologers moved into India, too.

Russia, on the contrary, got the seven-day week a little later from Christian missionaries, who refused to say the names of the days. That is why most of the week days are still spoken of by numbers, instead of names, in the Russian, Polish, and Czech languages.

The week went to China also with missionaries. They

introduced it there without the planetary names (which they regarded as superstitious). So in China now people call the days, "of the week, one," "of the week, two," "of the week, three," and so on.

But Japan got the week much later from Dutch missionaries, who did use the names. So in Japanese the days are now called by the Japanese names of the seven planets.

The story of the week in Iceland is extraordinary. The first settlers in Iceland were Teutons who brought with them the seven-day week just as they had learned it from the Mithraist Roman soldiers. The Icelanders also brought the old Teutonic religion. They worshiped Woden, Thor, Frigg, and the other northern gods.

And Iceland was one of the last countries in the western world to be Christianized. The people were converted between 1000 and 1100. They then suddenly changed their ideas about the days of the week. They dropped the old names. Tuesday, Wednesday, Thursday, Friday had been Tiu's day, Woden's day, Thor's day, and Frigg's day (in their language: *Tysdagr*, etc.). Suddenly these days became third day, mid-week day, fifth day, and fast day. But the name for Saturday is still Mithraist: *Laugardagur*, which means "bath day."

So now the seven-day week has become customary almost everywhere in the world. About half the nations use the planetary names, as we do in English.

SUN

Sunday

WHEN THE Teutons were translating the names of the days of the week into their language (the ancestor of English) they had no trouble with *dies Solis* (the day of the sun).

The Mithraist Roman soldiers said prayers to the sun on that day. To the Teutons, who hunted and fought in the forests of Germany this practice seemed reasonable, for they too said prayers to the sun, especially on the longest day of the year (in June) and on the shortest day (in December).

And those Teutons often chipped out a stone image of the sun. They called it their "sun wheel." It was a spiral patterned disk. When they could, they covered it thinly with hammered gold. Sometimes they carved a wagon under it and a horse in front of the wagon.

These images were explained by a story.

Once upon a time there was a man named Turner (in their language, Mundilfari) who had a huge, bushy beard and two very good-looking children. The children were so fair and handsome that he called his boy Moon and his daughter Sun. He was a stuck-up father. Lovingly he stroked the girl's yellow hair and patted the boy's broad shoulders. He taught them to stand up straight, and made them run, jump, and wrestle, so that they would grow to be strong. And he boasted to everyone, "My children are more handsome than the gods!"

So the gods became angry at him. Woden said, "He is too proud. What right has he to call his boy Moon and his girl Sun?"

Woden and Tiu took the children away from him and carried them off to heaven. There the gods gave these young people hard tasks to perform.

To the boy, Woden said, "Now you shall mount upon the wagon of the moon, and you shall control the moon's great horse and drive it across the wide dome of heaven. When the lamp of night is young you shall ride down the western sky soon after sunset. Each evening thereafter you shall ride longer, till when the moon is full you are to drive your wagon up the eastern sky just at sunset and light the world all night long."

To the strong young girl, Tiu said, "Now you shall mount upon the wagon of the sun, and you shall control brave Shining Mane, his horse. Each morning you shall make him bring forth the glittering day. Be not afraid of him, though brightly his mane burns. For now we entrust to you the sun, this great burning disk, which the gods have made to light the world."

The girl named Sun looked wonderingly at the proud horse and the fiercely gleaming fire disk. "Does not the horse become overheated from galloping so close ahead of the sun?" she asked.

But the gods laughed at her ignorance. Then they showed her the two bellows built under the shafts of the sun car. As the wheels turned, the bellows worked, blowing air on the horse to keep it cool.

Then the boy mounted upon the wagon of the moon, urged on his horse, and rose across the night sky. Boldly he steers the glowing orb, the gleamer, the teller of time, the moon that the gods have made.

And the girl mounted upon the wagon of the sun, urged on her horse, and rose across the sky, bringing the day to all men.

Thereafter each night and day the round of heaven they run.

When the Roman soldiers heard this story, they pointed out that according to Mithraism the sun rode in a chariot drawn by four horses.

At this news the Teutons looked skeptical. They had no chariots, only wagons.

However, after they had seen Roman chariots, they naturally let their flaming disk of the day ride in a chariot of the latest model. But they never could quite believe in those four horses. Later Scandinavian poets gave the sun two horses. But four?

In Mithraist doctrine the sun chariot was driven by a

mighty god (not a girl). He was a god of many names: Helios or Apollo or Sol or Shamash. And he was strange and wonderful. He was a god, but also he was the sun, and at the same time he was only an ideal.

Mithras fought the sun god, then became his brother. And, just as Christianity has its mysteries, such as God the Father, God the Son, and God the Holy Spirit, who are three and yet are one, so also Mithraism had its mysteries. Mithras and the sun were two. They also were one. Mithras was the brother of the sun. He also was the sun.

Therefore the worshipers in that cult made many statues of the sun god (Helios or Apollo or Sol or Shamash) in his four-horse chariot. The most famous was the Colossus of Rhodes, which was 120 feet high. And that really is high—like a ten-story building. It was erected on the island of Rhodes in 280 B.C. (But it did *not* stand with its legs astride the harbor, as some people said.)

With these beliefs, we can see why the Mithraists considered Sunday very important and had special ceremonies that day.

One of their ideas gave us a particularly popular custom.

The priests told the people that the sun was made of fire and that water is the enemy of fire. Therefore you must not bathe or wash with water on the sun's day. On the other hand, the Mithraists were great sticklers for cleanliness and always made great efforts to keep from being dirty. So they must be clean on Sunday. But how?

There was only one solution to this problem: they had to bathe every Saturday night.

Some of the Teutons took up this custom enthusiastically. (The name for Saturday became "bath day" in several of their dialects. In modern Swedish and Danish the word for Saturday still is *Loerdag* and in Icelandic it is *Laugardagur*, meaning "bath day.")

Dies Solis (the day of the sun) was easily translated as *Sunnundag*, which means the same. The tribes who went to England gradually changed it to *Sunnandaeg* and then to *Sunday.*

Is Sunday the Sabbath?

The *Encyclopaedia Britannica* article on "Sunday" starts off boldly: "Sunday—The Lord's day in the Christian world, the first day of the week—"

The first day? But some calendars printed in Europe show Sunday as the seventh day. In the Russian language and in Polish, Czech, and Chinese the words for Tuesday mean "second day," which makes Sunday not the first but the seventh day.

And the Bible says God created the world in six days, and on the seventh day he rested. Obviously the Sabbath is the seventh day.

So who is right?

If we study the history of the Sabbath, we can learn which is right.

In the first place, when the astrologers gave the week days the names we now use, they began with the day of the sun because that was the most important planet. And they ended with the day of Saturn because it was an unlucky planet, whose day had to correspond to the Babylonian "seventh day." That had been a day of taboos ever since the earliest times that their records could tell of.

When the Hebrew leaders returned from Babylon after their captivity and took with them the book of Genesis, they had their own kind of week, as we have seen, called first day, second day, third day, fourth day, fifth day, sixth day, and Sabbath. The Hebrew word was *Shabbath*, meaning "day of rest." They celebrated it on the same day as the Babylonian "seventh day" and the astrologers' day of Saturn.

Therefore, so far as the Jews are concerned, the seventh day has always been Saturday.

What about the Christians?

During the lifetime of Jesus, he and his followers worshiped with the other Jews on Saturdays in the synagogues.

Two difficulties made them change to Sunday.

In the first place, as they were not satisfied with the prayers and sermons of the rabbis, the earliest Christians soon got in the habit of meeting twice. They met on Saturday because it was the Sabbath, and again the following day because they wanted additional prayers and sermons of their own.

And, in the second place, they ran into differences of opinion about the strict Sabbath laws.

Some of the scholarly Jews, especially the sects called Pharisees and Sadducees, had elaborate laws against work on that day. What was work? It included plowing, reaping, gathering wood, lighting a fire, cooking—also it included carrying any burden or even loading an animal. The laws also forbade traveling, writing, or curing sick people. Scholars argued over such details as how much could you carry before it was a burden? The stricter ones decided you must not carry anything that weighed as much as a fig. Anything less was permitted. Anything more was forbidden.

How much reaping was reaping? They said you were allowed to pluck one ear of wheat on the Sabbath, but not two ears.

If your house caught fire on the Sabbath you could not carry things out of it. You could put on a lot of extra clothes, run outside, and take them off, then run in and put on some more. But you must not *carry* them out.

Most of the poor people could not take time to learn all the rules and would not obey them anyway. If they needed to carry a burden, and the day happened to be the Sabbath, they carried their burden.

In this difference of opinion, Jesus sided with these poor people against the scholars. (I am taking this from *The Catholic Encyclopedia* article on "Sabbath," if you want to check it. I have also seen it in many other books.) When his disciples were hungry on a Sabbath day and were walking through a wheat field, he allowed them to pick ears of wheat and eat them, although some Pharisees, who saw it, protested.

In defiance of the law he cured sick people on the Sabbath. He even told one, "Take up your bed and walk." Assuming it was a light bed—perhaps only a roll of blankets—even so, it weighed much more than a fig, and the scholars were shocked.

88

At first the early Christians continued going to religious services on the Sabbath in spite of their disagree-
ment about these rules. But the arguments between them
and the Pharisees became gradually more and more
heated. The early Christians continued to meet the following day also (Sunday).

Eventually they were expelled from the synagogues.
They were shoved out at different times in different
places, from A.D. 50 to A.D. 90.

Then they met elsewhere, sometimes next door to a synagogue. But gradually most of them dropped the Saturday meetings and concentrated on Sundays.

Some did not make the change. Many eastern Christians continued for centuries to worship both on Saturday and on Sunday. Those in Ethiopia still do.

And, finally, it was said that Jesus was crucified on a Friday, and on the following Sunday he was raised from the dead. He then visited some of his apostles before going up to heaven. Most churches honored his resurrection every Sunday. In the Russian language now the name for Sunday is a word meaning Resurrection Day.

But is Sunday the Sabbath? In the first three centuries of Christianity preachers wrote emphatically again and again that it was not. They said that anyone guilty of "sabbatizing"—keeping the Bible rules about the Sabbath—might be Jewish but he certainly was not Christian.

However, they said that to rest one day a week was a good idea. And if you had slaves or other people working for you, it was humane to let them rest on Sundays. But the early Christians refused to have any laws about it. They remembered too bitterly the revolt of Jesus and his disciples against the Sabbath laws.

But then Constantine became Christian and emperor of the huge Roman Empire. He had his own ideas. He issued decrees (in A.D. 321) forbidding people to work on

Sundays. He did not make any other Sunday blue laws, only that people should not work.

The Christian church did not know quite what attitude to take toward this emperor. Three or four writers tried a new approach. They suggested that Christ had transferred the Sabbath and the Bible rules about it from Saturday to Sunday. However, there is nothing in the Bible to say that he did. The church frowned on this idea, and the Catholic Church is still against it.

Much later, in England in 1558 at the time of the Protestant Reformation, this idea was revived. Some Protestants began calling Sunday the "Sabbath" and made many laws about it. In that year a law said that everyone in England must go to church on Sunday or be fined twelvepence.

Both in England and in America many laws were made forbidding people to play games on Sunday or dance or listen to music or get drunk or to buy or sell anything.

Contracts still are sometimes not valid if signed on a Sunday or if worded in such a way that they are to take force on a Sunday. For instance, if you agree to deliver a turkey to Mr. Jones on March 16 and that day turns out to be a Sunday, your contract is technically no good in some states. But I never heard of anybody's refusing to accept a check made out on a Sunday.

The Catholic Church still takes the stand that most of these laws were mistakes. It points out that the Sabbath is Saturday, the Jewish day of worship. It says that the Old Testament rules about what you must not do on the Sabbath do not apply to Christians.

However, most churches still say (as the early Christians did) that you ought to attend divine services on Sunday and that it is humane to rest and especially to let your employees rest at least one day a week.

Even the Arabs, whose day of religious worship is Friday, call Sunday the first day and Saturday the Sabbath.

Many scholars now agree that the people who at one time called Monday the first day and Sunday the seventh, simply made a historical error. (That way of counting, however, still exists in the Russian, Polish, Chinese and other languages in which Tuesday, for instance, is called "second day.")

As for the word *Sabbath*, some Protestants still use it for Sunday, but most do not. And Catholics are definitely not supposed to.

Sunday schools for children are a fairly recent invention, and they began in America.

They were first organized on a large scale by John Wesley in Savannah, Georgia, in 1737.

In New York, however, a smaller Sunday school had been put in operation ten years earlier. Anna Zenger seems to have invented the idea. She was the wife of the famous printer, Peter Zenger, who first established freedom of the press in America. One evening she stood up before a business meeting of the elders of the Dutch Reformed Church. They seemed very solemn in their black coats and broad white collars. She told them it was a pity to see children squirming restlessly in church during the long sermons, so bored that they were learning nothing about religion. So the elders granted her a little money to assemble a few other mothers of the parish and teach the children separately on Sundays.

After John Wesley's work the custom spread very widely in America and in England. At first, however, it was chiefly a means of teaching poor children to read and write.

Then around 1880 several nation-wide Sunday school organizations were formed and began printing regular weekly lessons on religion. These inexpensive printed sheets made the work of untrained Sunday school teachers much easier. It was these printed lessons that really made Sunday schools a regular part of American life. (They still are much less common in other countries.)

Sunday Round the World

Sunday was called simply "first day" by the Hebrews, who refused to give it any name. But in the following ancient languages it was given names meaning either "sun" or "day of the sun":

BABYLONIAN	SHAMASH
IRANIAN (PERSIAN)	HVAR
GREEK (CULT OF MITHRAS)	HELIOS *or* APOLLO
SANSKRIT	RAVIVARA
LATIN (CULT OF MITHRAS)	DIES SOLIS
TEUTON	SUNNUNDAG
ICELANDIC	SUNNUDAGR

The early Christians called it "Lord's day":

GREEK	KURIAKOS
LATIN	DIES DOMINICA

The following are modern names. Most have grown from these ancient ones.

From the Mithraist Latin *dies Solis* ("day of the sun") :

WELSH	DYDD-SUL

From the Teuton *Sunnundag:*

ENGLISH	SUNDAY
GERMAN	SONNTAG
DUTCH	ZONDAG
SWEDISH	SOENDAG
DANISH	SOENDAG
MODERN ICELANDIC	SUNNUDAGUR

94

SUNDAY

These also mean "day of the sun":

BENGALI	RABIBAR
TAMIL	YNAYIRU
JAPANESE	NICHIYOBI
ALBANIAN	DIELLI

From the Christian Latin *dies Dominica* ("Lord's day"):

FRENCH	DIMANCHE
ITALIAN	DOMENICA
SPANISH	DOMINGO
PORTUGUESE	DOMINGO
GAELIC-IRISH	DI-DOMHNAICH

From the ancient Greek *Kuriakos* ("Lord's day"):

MODERN GREEK	KIRIAKI

Other modern names for Sunday:

RUSSIAN	VOSKRIESIENIE	("Resurrection
HUNGARIAN	VASARNAP	day")
POLISH	NIEDZIELA	
CZECH	NEDELE	("not working")
BULGARIAN	NEDELYA	
CHINESE	LI-PAI TIEN	
	("of the week, the day")	
ARABIC	YOM EL HADD	
	("the first day")	

95

MOON

Monday

WHEN THE Teutons translated the names of the days of the week, they did not hesitate over *dies Lunae* (the day of the moon).

The idea that the Mithraist Roman soldiers should offer a prayer or two to the moon now and then seemed to them reasonable.

Although the Teutons did not have any formal calendar, they did hold their tribal assemblies on the days of the new moon and of the full moon.

When the warriors and chiefs got together on one of those days, they sometimes held a religious ceremony, combined with a big feast with lots of ale to drink. Other times on these meeting days they had their popular assembly—called their "ding"—which was their government.

In addition to the ding, each tribe had a chief or king. A man became chief or king not because his father had been but because he himself could talk in the ding and persuade the others to vote for what he thought they should do. Of course, he had to do more than talk. He also had to be a good fighter, a good hunter, and a good thinker for making plans, as well as a skilled leader to go personally and direct a hunt or a battle.

If he was known as a real man—a man who could do all these things—the other warriors would listen to him in the assembly.

They were not good listeners. When they met—in the woods, or at a temple when they had a temple—they were very noisy. If a speaker did not interest them, or if he was known to be a coward, they would boo and whistle and laugh, till he could not be heard.

Voting was not done quietly either. It was done by shouts. When the warriors became angry and voted against some project that displeased them, they banged their swords on their shields and yelled and made such a racket that they frightened animals and birds half a mile away.

When an assembly broke up, they often said to one another, "We'll meet again next month." Without a written calendar, how did they keep count of the days of a month?

They could barely read and write. At this period (from A.D. 100 to 200) they were slowly developing a system of runes. A small party of Teuton warriors had recently wandered down into northern Greece, where they had seen Greek writing. Although they had not understood it, they

came home and made an alphabet that looked something like it. Their letters were called runes. By means of runes each man could scratch his name on his weapons. A few of the leaders collected magic spells cut on slabs of wood in that alphabet. But they had no books, no written manuscripts, no regular method for writing down any news about the days that passed.

So the moon was their calendar. The next assembly would be at the next full moon—or the next new moon, if they wished. For urgent business they occasionally met at the half moon, too. Since these phases occur every seven or eight days, we might say the Teutons had weeks. Well, anyway, a sort of week.

They called the moon the Teller of Time. And, from gratitude, men said a few prayers to it.

They believed that the boy named Moon drove the Gleamer, the Wheel, the Goer, the Teller of Time in a wagon across the sky. And eclipses were caused by great wolves who chased after him, trying to eat the moon. Luckily the wolves have never yet succeeded. Sometimes they come close enough to take a bite or even to take the whole thing in their mouths. But so far they never have been able to swallow it and always they have had to spit it out.

However, some day—at the time of the Twilight of the Gods—two extra big wolves will get loose in the sky. One will eat the sun, the other the moon. And then the long darkness will begin. No warmth of sun or light of moon will come to cheer men's world. Three winters will follow, one right after another, with no summers in between.

But the Teutons at first thought the Mithraist Roman

soldiers must be weak in the head to say prayers to the moon every *dies Lunae* when usually that day was not the day of a full moon nor a new moon nor a half moon.

Which were right, the Teutons or the Mithraists? We have become so used to measuring days, weeks, and months entirely on paper that some of us (like the Mithraists) forget to look up in the sky. The tough, loud-talking, hard-fighting Teutons enjoyed looking at the Gleamer, the Teller of Time. They thought it was pretty.

At least the name of the day was easy for them to translate. They called it *Monandag*. And after it went to England it gradually changed to *Monday*.

The Earliest Weeks

That system of agreeing to meet next at some phase of the moon was the easiest and most ancient way. It had begun when very primitive people worshiped the crescent moon only. Many African tribes and the people of Madagascar did this. (But the early Mexicans worshiped the full moon only. People don't all do things exactly alike.)

The ancient Javanese and the Tonkinese (in Vietnam) worshiped both new and full moons. It is surprising how many ancient peoples did this. Later some added the growing half moon.

In China about 2800 B.C. the king decreed that on the seventh day "the gates of the great road shall be shut and traders not permitted to pass, nor princes to go to examine their states." Of the twenty-eight constellations through which the moon passed in a month, each seventh constellation was marked (in the Imperial Almanac) "closed."

Traces of this old system of counting by moon phases have been found also in Burma, India, Persia, Babylonia, Arabia, Egypt, ancient Greece, and ancient Druid England. And in Peru and among the American Indian Mound Builders and in Hawaii.

The earliest Roman calendar had each month beginning on the day when the new moon was first seen. On that evening the priests called the people to tell them that another month had begun. So the first day of each month was the calends ("the calling"). That is where we get our word *calendar*.

Seven days later the nones was the day of the half moon. Eight days after that was the ides, or full moon. (I am referring to the early centuries before all this was made formal and meaningless.)

How the Old System Worked

The Teutons were counting time by a system so old that it had been used all round the world long before anybody had made those discoveries in astronomy which we discussed near the beginning of this book.

Before they knew anything else of astronomy, people caught on to what the moon does.

A modern almanac will tell you that the first phase is the new moon. Perhaps that is a silly name, for it is the day when we cannot see the moon at all. Ancient people called it the day of the dark of the moon.

On that day the moon rises and sets at almost the same moment as the sun. (Once in a while on that day it lands in exactly the same spot in the sky where the sun is. Then it causes an eclipse of the sun. Sun eclipses occur only on the day of the dark of the moon.)

A day or two later we first see the moon, a thin crescent, still close to the sun, going down in the west immediately after sunset. This is the day the ancient peoples used to call the Day of the New Moon. On this day the Hebrews and Babylonians and many others used to have celebrations. On this day the earliest Roman priests called the people to announce the beginning of the month, and the word for "calling" in Latin was *calenda*.

Each night thereafter the moon just after sundown is a little higher in the sky and a little bigger than the night before, because each night it is farther from the sun. Each night it sets in the west about forty-five minutes later. I say "about," because Old Night Lamp staggers a little. Its motion is not quite regular. Its speed changes from day to day. Perhaps it is a little crazy. Or so the astrologers thought. That is one reason why they believed that anyone too much influenced by *Luna* (the moon) was a lunatic.

Any modern almanac tells us that the next phase is the first quarter. This is when we see the half moon. (Who is crazy, the moon or the makers of almanacs?)

As it has been moving eastward away from the sun day by day, the half moon is high in the sky at sunset. Now we have plenty of time to see it. It is bright enough to be seen in the afternoon. It shines all evening and sets about midnight. (This is its most irregular period; so it may set nearly two hours before or after midnight.)

The next few days, as it grows larger and moves farther eastward from the sun, it is in the eastern part of the sky at sunset.

You know when and where to look for the full moon. It becomes full by being on the opposite side of us from where the sun is. Therefore it rises on the eastern horizon when the sun is going down in the west. That is, it always rises within twenty-five minutes before or after the sun sets.

One evening when I was on shipboard in the Mediterranean a lady came into the ship's lounge about 9 P.M. and said eagerly, "The full moon is shining over the water, and it's perfectly beautiful! You must come and look! But hurry! It's down near the horizon already and will soon set."

Some of the people jumped up and rushed out to look.

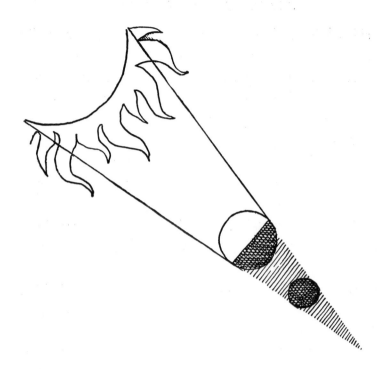

Would you have hurried? Can the full moon ever be setting at 9 P.M.? Even in the Mediterranean?

The full moon shines all night. If you get up before
dawn, you may see it setting in the west.

Many ancient peoples used to call that the day of con-
tinuous light—when the sun shines all day and the moon
all night. In winter in Germany both hunters and wild
beasts would prowl at all hours of that day and night.

(That also is the only time when an eclipse of the moon
can happen. Since what makes it full is its being on one

side of the world when the sun is on the exact opposite side, sometimes those three—the sun, the world, and the moon—line up very accurately, in that order. In fact, it happens fairly often. And then the earth's shadow falls on the moon, causing an eclipse.)

After the full, the moon continues to rise later each night—after sunset, and then later and later. Soon good people like you and me who go to bed at night do not see it any more.

The almanacs tell us that the last quarter rises about midnight. At sunrise it is high in the sky. All morning it is going down in the west, setting at noon. So you may see it at breakfast time, especially if the sun goes behind a cloud. And if you do, you will discover that it is a half moon.

Each day thereafter it becomes smaller and dimmer and closer to the sun. Being closer, naturally it rises nearer and nearer to the hour of dawn. Now it is too dim to be seen by daylight (except during a thunderstorm). Probably your only chance to see that last thin sickle moon will be if you get up before dawn.

If you *do* see it, please notice one thing about it. It is not a *crescent*. The word *crescent* means "growing." The thin sickle moon visible an hour or two *before* dawn is the waning moon. It looks like the crescent. But this thin waning moon is in the east. And you won't see it set. It merely fades out of sight when the sun comes up.

The end of the moon month is near. Soon the moon is again so close to that part of the sky where the sun is that they rise and set together. We are back to the day of the dark of the moon.

It has taken a little over 29½ days to go round. As it has four phases, a little arithmetic shows that each must come seven or eight days after the one before. Counting each phase as a week, here is an example of how long each one is. In three typical months (December, 1955, through February, 1956) the number of days in the moon weeks one after another were as follows: 7, 8, 7, 7, 7, 8, 8, 7, 7, 8, 7, 7.

A bit irregular. The advantage was that you could tell the day of the week just by looking at the sky. The disadvantage is obvious: you might have a hard time guessing how long the week after next was going to be.

How the Old System Died

For farmers moon weeks and months were a nuisance. Farmers had to plow and plant at the same time each year. In a warm climate they would begin in the second month of autumn. But the second moon month of autumn arrived ten days earlier each year than the year before. By the third or fourth year a farmer was likely to become confused about when to start work.

When people gave up trying to live entirely by hunting and they settled down seriously to farming instead, each nation had to do something about that old moon calendar. And each nation did something completely different.

In Babylonia, after giving a name to each lunar month of the year, the government solved the trouble very simply. Once every two or three years the king (when he felt like it) announced that there would be an extra month. He decreed that one of the months would be repeated; they would have April twice that year. By this means he made the autumn planting month arrive at about the correct season.

With this improvement in the old system, the Babylonians were able to keep it and also keep the lunar-week religious celebrations on the actual days of the new moon and of the full moon. For a long time they did not give up this system officially.

Unofficially, however, about 700 B.C. their astrologers invented regular seven-day weeks.

The Egyptians, annoyed by the lunar months, tried a different solution. In the year 4241 B.C., as I mentioned earlier, the Pharaoh decreed that every month would be thirty days, with five extra days after the twelfth month, making the calendar year 365 days.

This had three effects. First, it made the autumn planting month come at the same time each year (almost). Second, it got away entirely from counting either months or weeks by the moon. Having lost the lunar week, the Egyptians invented a ten-day week to take its place.

The third effect is something of a joke. As the Egyptian calendar had no leap years, it slid round—but slowly. In forty years the autumn planting month moved, so it arrived about ten days too soon. Well, that did not matter much. In forty years people forgot what the exact planting day had been, and simply made it a little later. Every 1,460 years New Year's Day slid all the way round—to autumn, to summer, to spring, and then to winter again. Who cared? Nobody lived long enough to worry about it anyway.

As the Romans were farmers, they too, had to fix their calendar. But, knowing very little about astronomy, they did not measure the year accurately, and they made a mess of it.

They named the months—giving them the same names we still use. And then they added a few days to some of them, but not enough. Still, this change cut the months loose from the moon. The first day of each month went on being called the calends, though it no longer came on the day of the new moon. The middle day was still the ides, and in between came the nones, but these no longer came at any particular phases of the moon.

Furthermore, as their calendar year was not the right length, various kings had to keep changing it again and again to try to make the autumn planting month come at about the right season.

The man who finally did correct it and made our calendar out of it was Julius Caesar. While he was in Egypt with Cleopatra he got the idea. He decided to stop the Egyptian year from sliding round—and to clean up the Roman calendar at the same time. So when he got back to Rome he issued decrees. He added so many days to the year 46 B.C. that it consisted of 445 days. That was a long year! Historians call it the Year of Confusion. By this means he pulled the Roman month of January round to the winter again, where it belonged. He decided to have it begin (that is, January 1, 45 B.C.) on the day when the Egyptian first month happened to begin at that time.

Caesar also added one important detail—a leap-year day every fourth year.

From then on the Egyptian and Roman calendars were the same. With a small correction made many centuries later, that is the calendar we use now. (It is not very good. Do you think we are smart enough to make it better?)

The ancient Greeks muddled along for centuries with lunar months and the old irregular lunar weeks, some seven days, some eight days.

About 700 B.C. when they were buying and selling things in Egypt, they copied the old Egyptian system and began using ten-day weeks.

The Chinese had dropped their lunar weeks much earlier. The Javanese shifted to five-day weeks. Other peoples tried three-day or six-day weeks.

The Babylonian astrologers were the only ones who ended up with seven-day weeks. They made these weeks entirely independent of months or years. And after them the Hebrews did the same.

Monday Round the World

These ancient names for Monday mean "moon" or "day of the moon":

BABYLONIAN	SIN (THE MOON GOD)
IRANIAN	MAH
GREEK (CULT OF MITHRAS)	SELENE
SANSKRIT	SOMAVARA
LATIN	DIES LUNAE
TEUTON	MONANDAG
ICELANDIC	MANADAGR

The following are modern names. Most have grown from these ancient ones.

From the Latin *dies Lunae*:

FRENCH	LUNDI
ITALIAN	LUNEDI
SPANISH	LUNES
WELSH	DYDD-LLUN
GAELIC-IRISH	DI-LUAIN

From the Teuton *Monandag*:

ENGLISH	MONDAY
GERMAN	MONTAG
DUTCH	MAANDAG
SWEDISH	MANDAG
DANISH	MANDAG
MODERN ICELANDIC	MANUDAGUR

MONDAY

Other modern names meaning "day of the moon":

BENGALI	SOMBAR
TAMIL	TINGAL
JAPANESE	GETSUYOBI
ALBANIAN	HANE

These mean "second day":

MODERN GREEK	DEFTERA
PORTUGUESE	SEGUNDA-FEIRA
ARABIC	YOM EL ITNEN

Others:

CHINESE	LI-PAI I ("of the week, one")
RUSSIAN	PONIEDIELYNEEK ⎫
BULGARIAN	PONEDELNEEK ⎪ ("day after
POLISH	PONIEDZIALEK ⎬ not working")
CZECH	PONDELI ⎭
HUNGARIAN	HETFO (meaning unknown)

From this list we see the confusion in the numbering of the days. Chinese calls Monday the first day, while the three languages above that call it the second day. It really is the second day of the week.

Tuesday

WHEN THE Teutons were translating the names of the days into their language, they puzzled a long time over *dies Martis* (day of the planet Mars).

The planet had been named originally Nergal, and Nergal had been the Babylonian god of war. The idea had been that the three highest planets—Mars, Jupiter, and Saturn—represented the government. Mars, being the quickest of these distant three, must be the war department.

So when the astrologers gave Latin names to the planets, naturally they chose for this one the Roman war god, Mars.

But in the forts along the Rhine the Mithraist Roman soldiers had difficulty picking a Teutonic god for the planet, because all the Teutonic gods—Woden, Thor, Tiu—were gods of war. Even Frigg, the principal goddess, was a goddess of war. However, she and these gods had other traits, too.

When the Roman soldiers first began to hear of these gods, they found that Tiu was a great fighter and hero; so they decided he was like their Hercules. Later—around A.D. 200—the Teutons convinced them that Tiu was *the*

SEVEN DAYS FROM SUNDAY

god of war (more so than the others). So they decided he was Mars.

This is a typical example of Mithraist logic, which made much of the surface qualities of things. They said the sun is made of fire. Water puts out fire. Therefore water is the enemy of the sun. Therefore you must not wash on the sun's day. Very logical? When they heard the story of Noah and the Flood, they interpreted it with the same kind of surface logic. The flood seemed to be an attempt to destroy mankind. Therefore it was sent by Ahriman, the Prince of Darkness. Following this idea, they mixed up the whole story.

Seeing a superficial resemblance between Tiu and Mars, they decided he was Mars. They never thought their way down into the real meaning of things, or they would have seen that Tiu was no more Mars than a watermelon.

But they and the Teutons together ended by translating the day of Mars as Tiu's day.

Who was Tiu?

Those hard-fighting northern tribes whom we call Teutons had a very manly religion. All their gods and goddesses were brave, muscular, full of vitality. Sometimes they had a wonderful sense of humor, too.

On the mountainsides of Scandinavia and in the forests of Germany the warriors built temples much like those in ancient Greece, except that the Teutons built of wood. Here the priest or leader kept a perpetual fire on a raised stone altar.

In the dim light you would see a large statue, usually carved of wood, with real armor and with ornaments of iron or gold. The god Woden was portrayed as an old, bearded fighter fully armed, wearing a bronze helmet. He was shown standing, about to hurl his heavy spear, and accompanied by two wolves. The powerful god Thor stood in a wagon, his great hammer in one hand. Tiu, god of war and of government, carried a huge sword.

On festival days men paraded to the temple, marching in line, wearing fine clothes, blowing horns, singing. (When they had no temple, an altar in the woods was made to do.) They led bulls, horses, pigs (especially pigs) to the altar, slaughtered them ceremoniously, and collected their blood in a bowl. Then with a brush the priest, mumbling a prayer, solemnly sprinkled a little on the worshipers. (The word for this ceremony was *bloedsian*, meaning "to consecrate with blood." We still use the same word, which we spell *bless*.) Then they sacrificed part of the meat to the gods, and cooked the rest. They hung kettles over fires in the middle of the temple.

Then the men sat on benches along the walls. They put tables in front of them and ate noisily, with much laughter and much drinking of ale. They all drank a toast to Tiu and prayed, "May our leader lead us to victory! May he rule among us long and wisely!" They drank to other gods and prayed for peace, for plentiful harvests, and for protection against blizzards. They drank to any relatives who had died, and prayed for them.

After the feast they heard a harpist sing ballads about the gods. Then the hunters and warriors danced, standing in a line or in a circle round the fire, till it was time to go home.

This was a religion for fighting men. They felt stronger and braver from having feasted manfully in the house of their gods. Their temple was for making sacrifices to try to calm the unknown powers of winter storms. It was also for feasting, for boasting, for having a good time, so that afterward you could hunt or fight better.

When they felt worshipful, they turned their faces upward. In those lands of snow and of forests creaking in the wind the huntsmen marveled at the force, the power, the unexpected suddenness of all that was in the sky. The thunder, the tempest, and the bright sky itself were the principle objects of their fear and admiration. And in autumn they looked anxiously toward the sun, as it hung lower and lower in the chilly sky and the brief daylight was shorter every day, as though threatening to disappear forever. Men said prayers then, begging the sun to come back. At Christmas, when it had begun to return, they

dragged in a grand yule log, made a big fire, and enjoyed a special feast of celebration for the sun.

And the moon, of course, excited these sky-loving people. They held their assemblies when it was new or full.

They gave names to these and thought of them as gods: Thor (the thunder), Woden (the wind), Tiu (the sky), and the sun, and the moon. And every man has a mother, and most like to have a wife; so they added one more: Frigg the fair one, the goddess wife and mother.

This explains why they had six principal gods. When they named the seven days of the week, they were short one god. That is why Saturday still has the Roman name.

Also they believed in many spirits: the frost giants, the forest dwarfs, the water sprites—dozens of them. And as the tribes wandered, they picked up other gods from strange peoples whom they met. None of these was so important to them as their six principal gods.

In very ancient times the ancestors of these people had lived a little farther south in Europe. And some (the Achaeans) had gone down and conquered Greece.

The name of their chief god, ruler of the sky, meant "the bright-shining one." In three dialects it was pronounced Tiu, Tziu, and Dziu. If you try saying these aloud you can hear why they became Tiu, Zeus, and Ju. In Latin he was Ju the father, that is, Ju Pater or Jupiter.

As chief god he taught people the art of government. Zeus in Greece and Jupiter in Rome represented the ideal of the good king, president, or senator. And when the Roman government became very bad, people stopped believing in Jupiter.

Tiu, in Germany, was the god of the popular assembly (the ding). And, as the popular assembly frequently planned wars (apparently the Teutons loved to fight), he was also the principal god of war. Like Zeus in Greece, Tiu was the bravest of the gods, as we can see in the following story.

All these peoples kept making up stories about their gods. The stories about Zeus became different from the stories about Jupiter. The Teutonic poets told this story about Tiu.

Tiu and the Wolf

In the damp green forest the gods found an enormous gray wolf cub, snarling alone among the trees. He was much bigger than young wolves ought to be. Already each of his paws was as big as a man's fist.

The gods Thor and Tiu stood staring at him in amazement.

Thor said, "This is no beast to leave wild in the woods. What shall we do with him?"

In the dappled forest sunlight the wolf stalked round them, stirring up the old fallen leaves with the swish of his heavy tail.

Tiu wrinkled his war-scarred face. "Better to keep danger near than to leave it loose where it may surprise us. Let us lead him home."

So the gods led the wolf to Valhalla, the high hall of old god Woden. Woden stroked his beard uneasily as he eyed the strong shoulders of the young beast.

Then the wind god, skilled in magic lore, consulted a head that he kept in his dining room. (It was a wise man's head that had been chopped off, and Woden kept it and fed it and asked it questions.)

The head warned him, "This is no ordinary wolf, but a monster. His name is Fenrir. He is destined some day to destroy you. This the Fates have decreed."

The gods would not attempt to kill Fenrir, for any decree of the Fates must be respected. Also, Woden's home, Valhalla, was a sacred refuge. Nothing could be killed there.

So the wolf was allowed to run wild among the homes of the gods. Mostly he hid in the deep woods. On moonlit nights he would howl so dismally that men all over the world heard him and shuddered.

When he was hungry he would come to the gods and beg for food. But he was so fierce and so strong, snarling and snapping at everything around him, even biting branches when he was angry and yanking them off the trees, that none of the gods dared go near him—except Tiu. Tiu was the bravest god who had ever lived. Fearlessly he fed the wolf.

But the gods saw Fenrir growing altogether too rapidly. The young wolf's strength became alarming.

Woden called the gods to council and spoke before them. "Fenrir is fated to work us much harm. What can we do to hold him from us at least till that day of doom?"

So the gods approached Fenrir. Falsely smiling, they said, "Fenrir, let us play together."

Fenrir told them he would enjoy their company.

When they had run through the woods together in a friendly way and had come to a lonely place, the gods said, "Fenrir, show us how strong you are. Let us put this leather strap round you and see if you can break it."

Fenrir, eager to show off his great strength, meekly let them put a thick leather strap round him and tie it to an enormous oak tree. Then he lunged forward and broke the strap.

So the gods prepared a mighty chain. Again they approached the wolf. "Fenrir, show us how strong you are.

Let us put this round you and see if you can break it."

Fenrir, smiling and slobbering with his great, red mouth, meekly let them put the chain round him and fasten it to an enormous rock. Then he lunged forward, straining his great muscles. And the chain broke.

The gods began to worry.

Woden went to a dwarf, who was the most skillful workman in the world. "Dwarf," he asked anxiously, "can you make us a chain stronger than any in the world? We have great need for it."

The ugly little dwarf rubbed some of the smoke off his face. "Yes, I can," he answered, "if you bring me the necessary materials."

Woden promised, "Only name what is needed. We will bring them."

The dwarf demanded, "Bring me six things: the noise of a cat's step, the beards of women, the roots of mountains, the nerves of bears, the breath of fishes, and the spittle of birds."

Woden nodded. "Very well, you shall have them. They all are things the world can get along without."

And with these materials the dwarf made a chain stronger than any in the world. But it was as light as thistledown and as soft as silk.

The gods tried pulling on it but could not break it. Smiling, they went once more to play with Fenrir.

This time, when the wolf saw the chain and noticed

how soft and light it was, he became suspicious. He asked, "If the chain remains unbroken, do you agree to release me?"

They said, "Oh, we are all friends. Do you not trust us? We just want you to try your strength on this."

Fenrir replied, "If I cannot free myself, I may wait long to be released by you."

The gods taunted, "Are you afraid?"

Fenrir bristled and answered them again. "You shall not accuse me of lacking courage. Come, let one of you place his hand in my mouth as a pledge of your sincerity. Then I will consent to test your new chain."

The gods stood looking at one another. They shrugged and stroked their chins in doubt.

Grinning savagely, the wolf returned their taunt to them, "Are you afraid?"

None was bold enough to take such a risk—except Tiu. As he was not afraid of anything, he stretched forth his hand and placed it within the jaws of the beast.

Quickly the gods tied the soft chain about the shaggy neck and shoulders. It was so light, it lay like dew on the tips of the wolf's fur. They secured the other end of the chain to a huge rock and put a mighty boulder on top of that.

Fenrir lunged forward. But the new chain did not break. Straining his great muscles, he tugged and struggled. The chain only became tighter.

Tiu tried to pull away his hand, but the wolf kept a firm grip on it. "Let go my hand!" cried Tiu. "You are biting me."

"Untie me, then," growled Fenrir.

But the gods began to laugh. They had no intention of letting the wolf go. So Tiu lost one hand.

Mad with rage, the wolf snapped and bit at everything round about. He roars horribly. The slobber running from his mouth makes a river. And there he will stay till the day of the doom of the gods.

We notice that when this story was put together (about A.D. 500) Tiu was no longer chief of all the gods. He had become less important than Woden. Why?

Tiu suffered one misfortune in the north. Down in Greece and Rome, where he was Zeus and Jupiter, he got the thunderbolt, but somehow in the north he never did. Among the Teutons Thor was the one who hurled the thunderbolt. Perhaps in the north there was so much thunder, the people needed a special god for it. Without the thunderbolt it was hard for Tiu to remain supreme.

At the time when the names of the days of the week were translated, people still prayed to Tiu at the opening of each popular assembly. As god of government, he was supposed to look over the discussion and the voting.

But Woden, god of the wind in those windy northern lands, was god of wisdom. So after a while people began to pray to him in the popular assembly, where wisdom was needed. By A.D. 500 (after Tuesday had been named for him) Tiu was pushed aside.

And if the poet who first made up that story about the wolf had deliberately tried to destroy Tiu, he could not have thought of a more effective way to do so.

At first people accepted the story. It was in character. It seemed to show a wonderful example of bravery.

But a god who risked his right hand backing a false promise was too silly for anyone ever to take him seriously again. After this story became attached to Tiu, his cult died out, and we hear very little more about him.

We are told that his father was wise and fierce and lived in a remote castle, where he had a kettle a mile deep. Tiu's mother was bright-browed and generous. But his grandmother had nine hundred heads, and Tiu loathed her. I think I don't like her much either.

Most of these stories were not written down until the years between A.D. 850 and 1050. By then all the stories about Tiu, except what I have told you, had been forgotten.

That is why, although he was so important that a day of the week was named for him, we almost never hear anything about him.

Poor Tiu!

127

Tuesday Round the World

Ancient names for Tuesday, meaning "planet Mars" or "day of Mars":

BABYLONIAN	NERGAL
IRANIAN	VAHRAM
GREEK (CULT OF MITHRAS)	ARES
SANSKRIT	MANGALAVARA
LATIN	DIES MARTIS
TEUTON	TIESDAG *or* DINGESDAG
ICELANDIC	TYSDAGR

The following are modern names. Most have grown from these ancient ones.

From the Latin *dies Martis:*

FRENCH	MARDI
ITALIAN	MARTEDI
SPANISH	MARTES
WELSH	DYDD-MAWRTH
GAELIC-IRISH	DI-MAIRT
ALBANIAN	MARTE

From the Teuton *Tiesdag* ("day of Tiu"):

ENGLISH	TUESDAY
SWEDISH	TISDAG
DANISH	TIRSDAG

TUESDAY

From the Teuton *Dingesdag* ("day of the ding"—because Tiu was god of the ding, the popular assembly) :

GERMAN	DIENSTAG
DUTCH	DINSDAG

These also mean "day of the planet Mars":

BENGALI	MANGALBAR
TAMIL	CHEVVAI
JAPANESE	KWAYOBI

These mean "second day":

RUSSIAN	VTORNEEK
BULGARIAN	BTORNEEK
POLISH	WTOREK
CZECH	UTEREK
CHINESE	LI-PAI ERH

(So we see that Chinese is not alone in this mistake.)

In these languages Tuesday is called "third day" (which it is) :

PORTUGUESE	TERÇA-FEIRA
MODERN GREEK	TRITI
MODERN ICELANDIC	THRITHJUDAGUR
ARABIC	YOM EL TALAT

WODEN

Wednesday

WHEN THE Teutons translated the names of the days of the week, they were puzzled by *dies Mercurii* (day of the planet Mercury). They had no god exactly like Mercury.

However, Mercury was the tireless one, the swift traveler. (That was why his name had been given to the fastest planet.) And their god Woden also was the tireless one, the swift traveler. Mercury was god of wisdom. Woden was god of wisdom.

Of course, Mercury and Woden were not alike in other respects. Mercury was a messenger of the gods. Woden was one of the chief gods (later he became *the* chief god). He was too important to be a mere messenger. Mercury was god of medicine. Woden, on the contrary, was god of slain warriors. So they were not really the same.

Nevertheless, because the two gods had at least a couple of superficial qualities in common, the Mithraists with their usual inaccuracy translated *dies Mercurii* as Woden's day.

Who was Woden?

Originally he was the wind. And he was the receiver

of all bold warriors slain in battle. Their souls were carried to his home, Valhalla, where they feasted through the ages with him.

Later, as the following stories show, he became god of magic, of runes, and of poetry. His name means "crazy like a poet." From being god of magic, he developed into god of wisdom. From being god of poetry, he developed into god of all noble, high thinking.

From being god of wisdom, he gradually went further. From about A.D. 400 to 500 he pushed Tiu aside as god of government. At that time the Teutons in Scandinavia began to have kings and princes and noble lords and ladies. These people took Woden as their favorite. It was they who made him chief god.

The stories that we have about Woden are mostly noble and poetical. Notice the fine phrases that people used in speaking of him. (The stories about Thor, as you will see in the next chapter, are mostly comical.)

Woden the Creator

Old was the age of the dawn of the gods, when no worlds were: neither sea's cool waves on the sand, nor earth nor heaven. The eye of Woden was amazed, seeing no green grass but only one yawning gap. And deep in that open gap a giant lay, old Ymir, the formless one.

Then did Woden peer over the edge, he and his brothers, great Vili and Ve. "Here is that out of which we may make a world," said Woden.

"If we slay him," said Vili.

"Let us do it," said Ve.

When they slashed old Ymir, and slew the huge, sour giant, so much icy salt blood flowed from him that they made of it the ocean. Then Woden eagerly and his two brothers with mighty hands broke up the body of Ymir. Of his flesh they fashioned our earth, and the mountains they made of his bones. The three gods lifted the level land, mountain and moor, for all men to dwell therein. His hair was the trees, his teeth the stones. And of his brain the gods built the baleful clouds to move on high.

Then the sun from the south warmed the stones of this earth, and the ground became green with leeks and grass.

So the gods, the holy ones, sought their assembly seats and held council. They gave names to midday and twilight, to morning and night, and to the wandering moon.

Those were the peaceful years, the days of laughter. For the mighty gods made temples high timbered. Building forges, they heated iron and beat out new tools, held with tongs under the hammer. High homes they had, and gold in plenty. And they played at dice and chess on fine tables. Oh, 'twas good to be a god in those days!

But one wet evening from the giant's world three sisters traveled, three hill-high maidens. Gloom rode in their grim faces, and their hair knew no comb.

"Lazy gods!" they cried together. "Play now and think not of years hereafter. For the happiness of gods is as gossamer. You smile in the morning, but when darkness falls, then too falls your doom."

The gods, the holy ones, again sought their assembly seats and held council. But before they could answer, the three doom-tellers had gone.

The gods in council decided, "We shall need warriors to fight on our side." So they sent Woden, the wise one, to make men and women.

He took an ash tree. Of it he made man. And he took an elm tree. Of it he made woman. As yet they had no souls nor sense nor heat. And their still limbs were of ghastly hue.

But with his wonder working he gave them souls. His kinsman, good Honir, gave them sense. And Lothur, god of fire, put heat in their bodies.

Lo! Man did move, and woman beside him. Their skin glowed with good color. Lifting their new voices, they gave thanks with joy for the love of living.

But again from the giants' world came the three sisters, the hill-high maidens. Gloom rode in their grim faces, and their hair knew no comb.

"Past is my name," said one.

"Present, I," said another.

And the third one said, "Call me Future."

Together they, mighty in wisdom, handed man the wooden slabs cut with runes, the magic signs.

Man and woman, reading the runes, saw then their fate. Laws for their sons the slabs of wood told, and the life allotted to each child, and the destiny of all mankind.

The Wisdom of Woden

The gods long remembered the entrance by magic of Gold-Might—she of the Vanir, the lesser gods—into Valhalla. They called her the shining-one, and to their homes she brought craving for gain. The wide-seeing witch, wise in magic, bemused their minds. She was the joy of evil women. Sly men made Gold-Might their chief.

But Woden, the high one, in anger jabbed her with a sharp spear and heaved her on the fire of the hearth of his hall. When from the ashes she leaped up alive, he burned her again. Three times burned, three times reborn, still she lives, shining Gold-Might.

And the lesser gods, the Vanir, came from the sea to claim her. Like the waves, without number, armed and warlike, shouting vengeance, they raged, crying, "Down with the halls of the holy ones!"

Then war was made on the earth, the first in the world. The gods formed their battle line. The Vanir attacked.

Rich was the war prize, the much-sought reward. The winners thereafter, they knew, would receive worship from men: in temple and town the fervent chant, the sweet-smelling sacrifice. For to the victor always comes honor, and the losers eat crusts in a corner.

Wildly the Vanir hurried the onslaught. And the fighting holy ones valiantly strove to defend their homes. The wall that girdled Woden's home was broken, and his field trod by the feet of the warlike Vanir.

Then did high Woden unleash his spears, hurling dread slaughter among them. At his onrush the two armies, gods and Vanir, shook. The battle line wavered, the field was half saved.

When night fell, stilling the battle shouts, the gods wearily, uneasily sought their assembly seats and held council.

Good Honir, the friendly, advised, "Let us seek peace, pay tribute in gold to the Vanir, quiet their anger."

In swelling rage then rose up Thor, the mighty one, son of Woden. Seldom Thor sits when he hears such words. "What coward's talk is this? Shall we let the base ones, the lesser gods, take our places of worship? By my ruddy beard and red-dripping sword, if the word is mine I say fight to the end! We will win all or lose all!"

Wisely between these two Woden cut straight the way. "Hostages we shall give," he decided. "And hostages we shall ask from them. Let all, both gods and lesser gods, be worshiped together, as justice demands."

So in the wise peace the great gods, the holy ones, set their hands to rebuilding their halls and the wall that girdled their fields.

And Woden, lover of magic lore, having heard of the wisdom of Mimir, went to visit that long-bearded water sprite. Approaching the waterfall over Mimir's cave, he called out, "A gift! Give a gift to a traveler!"

"That will I," Mimir grumbled at the cave mouth, "if you give me an equal gift."

"What would you have?"

"Your eye," Mimir demanded. "Either one is a treasure, and one I would have."

Then Woden received great gifts of wisdom, deep words. And one of his eyes lies always under the water, far under, in Mimir's wide-famed well.

The Home of Woden

Whenever men fought, one bold army against another, the Valkyries hovered over the battlefield. Beautiful and awful were they, the warrior maidens. Men called them the choosers of the slain, for they selected which fighters should fall.

And from among the dead they lifted up the heroes,

137

those who had perished bravely, facing the foe. The best of the fallen fighters they led fresh from the field in a wild ride on their neighing, winged steeds to Woden's home, Valhalla, the hall of the slain.

Mighty was the home of Woden, the place of joy, where he lived with his good wife, Frigg. Its rafters were spears. Its roof was made of shields. A painted wolf's head hung by the western door, and over it an eagle carved of wood. And mighty were the ghosts of men feasting at Woden's banquets. The Valkyries served them. They were not stingy in pouring drink for the brave. All will fight firmly, their hearts faithful to Woden, in the final battle at the doom of the gods.

Woden's home had a watchtower, from which he looked out over all the world. And Frigg, the fair one, watched with him.

From the east the icy river Slith slithered through noxious valleys, home of swords and daggers and sharp cold. Here were the homes of the evil spirits, the giants who bring disease and disaster, the enemies of the gods.

In the north in the dark fields a hall of gold rose from the ice, home of dwarfs, skilled in metal working. On the side of a volcano full of fire amid the snow, the dwarf king had his beer hall.

And at the Beach of Corpses, far from the sun, a cave mouth gaped, the damp mansion ruled by the goddess Hel. Her door faced north and let in no warming light.

Through a smoke hole above, drops of poison dripped in. And snakes crawled in and out and around the rock walls. Here was the home of those dead who had been treacherous men, oath-breakers, murderers, wife-stealers. A dragon sucked their blood, and wolves tore them.

Woden and the Poetic Mead

Woden wanted to go to the Old Giant's hall to get some of the magic mead, the wondrous fermented mare's milk. To any who drank it, it gave the gift of poetry.

But the Old Giant lived on the other side of a mountain. To go over or round it was dangerous, as the way lay all through giants' country.

Woden took a gimlet named Rati, the traveler, and began to bore a hole through the mountain. The mouth of Rati made room for his passage. It gnawed a space in the stone. With his magic lore learned from Mimir, wise Woden changed himself into a snake and slippingly slid through the hole.

At the Old Giant's hall he reassumed his manly shape. Then he avoided the Old Giant but made much sweet talk to the Old Giant's daughter. To get his will he spoke full many a word in the old one's hall. Smoothly he won the smiling daughter. 'Tis little a wise man lacks.

139

She made him sit on a golden stool and gave him the magic mead. All frothing he drank it and sipped it and lipped it and said, "It is marvelous mead!"

But a heavy foot shook the path to the door. " 'Tis my father!" she cried. "For your life, flee away!"

But Woden, who had not finished, thrust his face in the bucket again.

The door slammed. "Who are you?" the giant demanded.

Tipsily Woden tittered, "I am Bolverk, the evil-doer. Would you be my friend?"

The Old Giant roared and waved a huge spear.

Woden leaped from the stool, his mouth still full.

The Old Giant charged.

Woden changed himself into an eagle and flew away.

Astonished, the giant stood by the open door. "I suspect you have sported with one of the gods," he grumbled. "Know you not we are their foes?" Then he slapped his daughter in the face and sent her to bed without any supper.

As Woden in the shape of an eagle flew over the world, his mouth was so full of the magic poetic mead that a few drops fell to earth. That is why today a few men are poets, but not many.

Next day a troop of frost giants, the sour ones, spirits of evil, with mighty arms came to Valhalla and knocked on the door.

Woden, dressed now in his best clothes and looking very solemn, spoke to them severely.

The frost giants demanded, "What became of Bolverk, who stole the poetic mead? Did he come back here among the gods? Or did the Old Giant slay him?"

Woden looked surprised. "Bolverk? Bolverk?" he said. "There is no god here by that name."

Wednesday Round the World

Ancient names meaning "planet Mercury" or "day of Mercury":

BABYLONIAN	NEBO
IRANIAN	TIR
GREEK (CULT OF MITHRAS	HERMES
SANSKRIT	BUDHAVARA
LATIN	DIES MERCURII
TEUTON	WODNESDAG
ICELANDIC	OTHINSDAGR
	(because Woden in some Teuton dialects was called Othin)

The following are modern names. Most have grown from these ancient ones.

From the Latin *dies Mercurii*:

FRENCH	MERCREDI
ITALIAN	MERCOLEDI
SPANISH	MIERCOLES
WELSH	DYDD-MERCHER
ALBANIAN	MERKURRE

From the Teuton *Wodnesdag*:

ENGLISH	WEDNESDAY
DUTCH	WOENSDAG
SWEDISH	ONSDAG
DANISH	ONSDAG

These also mean "day of the planet Mercury":

BENGALI	BUDHBAR
TAMIL	BUDAN
JAPANESE	SUIYOBI

These mean "middle of the week":

GERMAN	MITTWOCH
MODERN ICELANDIC	MITHVIKUDAGUR
RUSSIAN	SRIEDA
BULGARIAN	SRIADA
POLISH	SRODA
CZECH	STREDA
HUNGARIAN	SZERDA

These mean "fourth day":

MODERN GREEK	TETARTI
PORTUGUESE	QUARTA-FEIRA
ARABIC	YOM EL ARBA

Others:

CHINESE	LI-PAI-SAN
	("of the week, three")
GAELIC-IRISH	DI-CIADAIN
	("day of the first fast")

This last one comes from the fact that the early Christians had two fast days a week: Wednesday and Friday. Nowadays Catholics still must not eat meat on Fridays, but most people have forgotten about fasting on Wednesdays.

THOR

Thursday

WHEN THE Teutons translated the names of the days of the week, *dies Jovis* (day of the planet Jupiter) became Thor's day.

On the one hand, Jupiter and Thor were not entirely the same. In Rome Jupiter was the king of the gods. He was the bravest. He was the god of government. He was the heavenly father, thought to be the ancestor of most princely families in Greece and Rome. In the north Tiu was the bravest. Tiu was the god of government. If the Teutons or the Roman soldiers had been scholars, they would have known that Jupiter was Tiu.

On the other hand, Thor and Jupiter did have many qualities in common. Both were gods of the thunderbolt. (Jupiter's thunderbolt was a zigzag piece of metal; Thor's was a hammer.) Both were gods of strength. They were helpers in war, defenders of people who worshiped them. Both were the gods who gave force to contracts and promises; Romans swore by Jupiter, Teutons by Thor. Both gods had fought battles against giants.

Consequently, although the choice of Thor for the day of the planet Jupiter was wrong, nevertheless it was fairly logical.

Who was Thor?

Thor, God of Strength

Thor was the most popular of the northern gods. He was so much loved that peasants kept on worshiping him for five hundred years after nearly all Europe had become Christian.

When they made carved and painted wooden statues of him they showed him in the prime of life, with big muscles in his arms, and with a red beard.

During any thunderstorm they imagined Thor riding through the clouds in a wagon drawn by two big goats. To grasp his hammer he wore heavy gloves made of iron. It was a magic hammer. When he hurled it through the air it struck with a blinding flash (it was really the thunderbolt) and then returned by itself to Thor's hand.

The peasants thought he blessed marriages. If a thunderstorm occurred during a wedding, that was good luck. And they believed that without thunderstorms their crops would not grow. (There is just a chance that this might be true.)

Thor was a friend of man, for he helped mankind against the demons and evil spirits, who were giants. Thor killed lots of giants. To him, giant-killing was a sport. He enjoyed it and laughed a good deal. Many of the stories about him are full of fun.

His hall was in Thruthvang (place of strength). His mother was the earth. His sons were Power and Courage, his daughter Might. (He quickly produced other sons whenever he needed them.)

Many temples were built to him, usually on the tops of hills. Then the whole hill was sacred. No one could go hunting there. Anyone in trouble could take refuge there, for it was forbidden to kill or beat anybody in the holy home of a god. Before the tribes had any law courts, the leader of the tribe and his councilors met at a temple and tried disputes or criminal cases.

In Thor's temple a large iron ring lay on the altar, because men came there when they wanted to swear an oath. If two leaders agreed to help one another in battle, they would take their men to Thor's temple, touch the ring, and make an oath on it in the presence of many witnesses. And in solemn ceremonies a priest wore this ring on his arm. (They thought it was big enough for Thor's finger.)

When Thor's Wife Lost Her Hair

One of Thor's companions was Loki, god of mischief. Sometimes Loki was a friend, sometimes an enemy. Probably he represented evil, which we always have with us. We never can get rid of it, as Thor never could get rid of Loki. The best we can do is control it. That is what the Teutons believed.

Once mischievous Loki sneaked up on Thor's wife, Sif, while she was sleeping and maliciously cut off all her long, beautiful yellow hair.

Sif was big, powerful, and handsome. But without any hair she really looked rather ridiculous. Angrily she stalked up and down Thor's hall, waving her fists and shouting for vengeance till the veins stood out on her bald head.

When the other gods saw her, they laughed. Woden clapped his hands to his belly and roared with laughter.

Thor did not see the joke. He had often laughed. But not this time. Frowning and clutching thoughtfully with one hand at his red beard, he looked round the hall with his shrewd, fighting god's eyes. He felt sure that whoever had committed this absurd theft would not be able to resist a desire to stay and watch the fun.

Sure enough, peeking from behind an overturned table was the bitter one, Loki, who was eying the laughers with an evil smirk on his wrinkled, twisted face.

148

Thor kicked aside the table and raised his hammer, roaring like an angry bull.

Loki leaped aside and crouched among a group of the gods. They scrambled out of the way, chortling and yelling, and left him alone.

"Kill me," Loki taunted. "Go ahead, kill me. What good will that do you? My death will not bring back Sif's hair. But you are too stupid to have thought of that. Kill me, and she shall be bald forever!"

Thor hesitated, resting his hammer on his shoulder. He pondered. Growling, he commanded, "I give you three days. Put new hair on Sif, as good as she had, or you die!"

"Anything you wish, of course!" snarled Loki. "But who can make hair like hers grow in three days?"

Thor raised his hammer again. "Get you gone to the dwarf king. Have him make hair for her of spun gold, fine and lustrous. You are clever. You find a way to persuade him!"

Seeing the hammer about to swing at him, Loki leaped through the open doorway and sped on his journey.

No one knows what witty device he invented to persuade the ill-mannered dwarf king. But three days later Loki appeared again, smirking in Thor's doorway.

With a mock solemn gesture he laid on Sif's head magic tresses of gold as fine as hair. In an instant she was lovelier than ever.

And from then on the new hair grew, always pure gold. Her servants fought one another for the loose strands on her combs. With one of those hairs the winner could buy kegs of ale and be drunk for a whole season.

Thor the Giant-Killer

Although Thor often fought the giants, he once went fishing with one of them.

On their way to the sea Thor happened to notice a herd of cows and bulls in a field. And he felt hungry. He was a tremendous eater. Sometimes when he felt hungry he simply could not control himself. So he killed two of the bulls and cooked them and ate them, all except the heads. He took the heads along with him for bait.

Thor and the giant rowed out in a boat. When they threw in their fishing lines, the giant caught a couple of whales, which he tied by a rope to the back of the boat.

Thor baited his hook with a bull's head and threw it in the water. After a few minutes he felt a bite and began to pull in his line. But he found he had caught the Midgard Serpent, which was so big it went all the way round the world and sometimes bit its own tail.

Thor was not frightened. He stood up in the boat and began to heave in his catch. He pulled so hard, the floor boards cracked under the pressure of his feet. Then the huge sea serpent jerked on the hook. Thor pulled harder. And his feet went right through the bottom of the boat. Fortunately his line broke, and the huge serpent swam away.

And Thor walked home along the bottom of the ocean, carrying the boat round his neck like a collar and dragging the two whales behind.

Once on a journey to the east Thor and his friend Honir the good and Loki and a couple of other companions got lost in a forest in the middle of the night. It was so dark they could not see among the trees but had to feel their way with their hands. However, they came to a house and found the door open. As the night was bitter cold, they went inside to get out of the wind.

Inside, the house seemed quiet and fairly warm. Tired from their long journey, the gods lay down to sleep.

But they had just begun to nod off when the whole house shook with an earthquake, and they were frightened by a terrific blowing noise.

Groping around in the house, they found a smaller room opening from the main one. As the smaller room seemed quieter and more sheltered, they went in there and soon were sleeping soundly.

In the morning, however, when they crawled out of their shelter, they found it was not a house but an enormous glove. The smaller room into which they had moved during the night was the thumb.

And beside the glove lay its owner, the great giant Skrymir. The earthquake had been caused by his rolling over in his sleep, and the terrific noise had been his snoring. They knew him well. Skrymir was the clever giant, sometimes called Utgartha-Loki, and had tricked them before.

Just then Skrymir awoke, sat up, rubbed his eyes,

yawned, and looked down at the gods. He smiled at them, thinking they were rather funny.

And the gods stood looking at one another in embarrassment, not knowing what to say.

Skrymir asked, "What are you doing here?"

"We have lost our way," Thor confessed.

So Skrymir said cheerfully, "Come with me. I will show you how to get out of the forest."

They walked all day but still were not out of the forest.

That evening Skrymir lay down in the darkness to sleep again.

By that time Thor was terribly hungry. The gods took out all the food they had with them and prepared to eat.

But Skrymir rolled over and saw them. "Oh, that looks good!" he cried in his huge voice. And he grabbed up all their food and put it in his wallet, which he fastened down with a great strap.

Then he stretched out again to sleep, and the night became pitch dark.

Thor yelled at him, "Give us our food!"

But the giant only chuckled and rolled about in the darkness, so they could not even be sure where he was.

"Give us our food!" roared the hungry Thor, "or I will smite you with my hammer!"

"Go ahead," chuckled the giant somewhere in the dark forest.

In a rage Thor hurled his hammer, which struck a distant tree with a loud crash. By its momentary light they saw the giant for an instant, rolling in the opposite direction. The hammer returned by magic to Thor's hand.

Thor hurled it again. It struck a rock with a deafening thud. By its momentary flash they saw the giant for an instant, rolling in a different direction.

Thor hurled the hammer a third time. It struck a distant hilltop with a dull boom. By its momentary light they saw the giant for the last time, rolling away in another direction, still unharmed and still chuckling.

That was the night when Thor went without any supper.

One reason why the peasants loved him was that he did not always triumph easily. Sometimes he was in trouble, as they often were. And, best of all, his troubles always were funny.

For instance, his fight with Hrungnir the giant.

Hrungnir had a heart that was a peculiar shape, with three horns, and it was made of stone. Also, his head was made of stone. He was very boastful and proud of his horse.

One day during a horse race this giant became overheated. Warm weather is particularly unpleasant if your head is made of stone. Seeing Thor's hall nearby, the giant rushed in, uninvited, grabbed up a large pot of ale, and drank it. As Thor liked ale and always had plenty of it around, the giant found some more and was soon thoroughly drunk.

At the sound of his roaring, Thor hurried home, found the giant licking soot off the ceiling, and shouted at him, "Out of my house! You stupid good-for-nothing!" Thor picked up a log of wood and hit the giant on the behind to make him hurry.

Hrungnir scrambled out through the doorway on hands and knees, then stood up, swaying, in the road. "You can't talk to me like that!" he scolded. "I challenge you to a duel!"

"I will gladly fight you if you wish," Thor answered. "You stand over there. I'll stand over here. Now, are you ready?"

The giant seemed uneasy. "What weapon are you going to use?"

"I will throw this hammer," Thor told him. "What weapon will you use?"

Then the giant realized that in the excitement of the horse race he had left his weapons at home. "Wait for me here. I must go arm myself."

"And do not come back," Thor advised, "if you are afraid."

"Who says I am afraid?" Hrungnir growled.

However, when Hrungnir reached home and picked up his weapon, which was an enormous grindstone, he felt all his courage slip out of him. He picked up his shield, which was of stone, too. But his courage did not return. He thought of asking some friends to help him. But he had so often boasted that he was stronger than any of his friends, they would probably laugh at him for asking them.

Then he thought of a better idea. Gathering a lot of clay and stones and plaster, he made a helper in the form of a dummy giant. He wanted to be sure that it would be big and frightening. So he made it taller than the highest hill.

But when he returned to the dueling ground, bringing his helper with him, Thor was not there. Thor had just had a baby son, who was then three days old. In the nursery Thor was playing with him, smiling, counting the boy's toes, and feeling very proud. Evidently this son was going to be extremely powerful, for he already— three days old—had huge muscles in his arms and shoulders. So Thor named him Magni, the Strong One.

Hrungnir the giant was roaring in front of the house, "Where is Thor? Let him come out and be smashed like a worm when I strike him!"

Thor's servant went to see who was making so much noise. There stood the giant, his stone head shining in the afternoon sunlight high above the trees, as he waved his grindstone in one hand and his stone shield in the other. The servant decided to test how stupid Hrungnir was.

"Be on your guard!" called Thor's servant. "Thor is about to strike you, though you do not see him."

The giant looked all around. He whispered anxiously, "Where is your master hiding?"

The servant put up a hand to cover his grin. "Thor is hiding under the ground. He will spring up right under your feet!"

"Oh, is that so?" the giant taunted. "I guess I am too smart for him!" And he laid his great stone shield on the ground and stood on it.

At that moment Thor, who had heard the rumble of the giant's voice, ran out of the house and saw him. And beside the giant—apparently—was another giant even bigger. "You cheater!" Thor shouted. "You challenged me to a duel, and now you bring a helper with you!"

Angrily Thor hurled his hammer as hard as he could.

Hrungnir had raised his grindstone to throw it, so it was near his ear. Thor's hammer struck the grindstone, shattered it to pieces, bounced off, and bashed the giant's stone head, which shattered in many fragments, too. Great hunks of stone were flying in all directions as the giant toppled over.

One of the chunks of the grindstone hit Thor. It knocked him flat. An instant later, as Hrungnir crashed to the ground with a thud like an earthquake, one of the giant's feet landed on Thor's neck.

Thor's servant, meanwhile, armed with a long spear,

rushed into the fight, too, and attacked the giant's helper. However, as this turned out to be only a dummy, the servant knocked it down without much trouble.

Hearing these tremendous thumps and crashes, the other gods came running to see what had happened. They were much pleased to find the haughty giant stretched on the ground, for he had given them a lot of trouble.

"Stand up," said Woden to Thor. "Let us congratulate you."

"I can't stand up," Thor pointed out. "This giant's foot is on my head, and it is as heavy as a hillside."

One after another the gods tried to lift the giant's foot off Thor's neck. But it was too heavy for them.

"What has happened to my father?" demanded a voice in the doorway.

Everyone turned to look. There stood Magni, three days old, flexing his muscles in the late afternoon sunlight. When he saw what the trouble was, he said, "Stand aside. It is the duty of a son to help his father."

Seizing the giant's foot by the heel, Magni picked it up, heaved it on his shoulder, and tossed it to earth.

That was the right kind of son for Thor to have.

One morning Thor woke up and yawned and stretched comfortably in bed. With one powerful arm he tossed off the huge woolly bedcover made of sheepskins sewed together. With the other hand he groped on the floor for his hammer, which always lay beside him while he slept.

He groped again. It was not there.

With a feeling of panic he plopped down on hands and knees and looked under the bed. He looked in all the corners of the room. No hammer.

Frowning terribly and growling with rage, he strode into the main room of his house. His servants had shoved the furniture aside, had sprinkled water on the floor, and were sweeping. One was stirring up the fire on the hearth in the middle of the room. But at the god's anger they all dropped their brooms and stared at him, wondering whether they should run away or come to his help.

He was aware that they all feared him. If they knew what had happened to his hammer they would not dare keep silent about it.

"Do you know anything?" he demanded.

"About what?" they asked, frightened.

He shrugged, stalked heavily to the front door, and looked out.

In the frosty morning light his old companion Loki was walking up the road toward him. Loki waved a greeting. But on the path in front of the door Thor saw enormous footprints, one set heading into the house, the other going away.

"Look at these," Thor said, as Loki approached. "And my hammer is gone."

Loki was astonished. All the wrinkles of his ugly face made circles around his open mouth.

"Whoever stole it would not dare stay here," Thor decided. "He is back in the giant realm by now. Shall we start after him?"

"You can't go there without your hammer," Loki pointed out. "Would you walk unarmed into the home of foes?"

Loki thought of a plan. "Let me borrow a flying suit, and I will go and spy on the giants."

Thor and Loki went to the fine, great hall of the goddess Freya. Although she was one of the Vanir, the lesser gods, she had come to live in the realm of the gods and had been accepted by them because she was the goddess of love and beauty. And she had a famous magic flying suit made of feathers.

With some difficulty they persuaded her to lend it. At last she said, "It is true that Thor must get back his hammer. Without it he cannot fight the giants, and they will destroy mankind. To help save mankind from them, I will lend you my flying suit."

Loki put on the suit and flew like a great, awkward bird over the mountains and into the realm of the giants.

There he passed several halls that seemed to be empty. Soon he came to one that was crowded. Dropping down

clumsily onto the roof, he tried to peek in through the smoke hole. He heard many voices of giants, all of them chuckling over some piece of good news. But so much smoke was coming out the hole that he could not see anything.

He waited till most of the giants had gone home. Then he descended from the roof and walked boldly in at the front door. He recognized the master of the place, a greedy giant named Thrym.

"Good day to you, Thrym," he said. "Have you any news of Thor's hammer?"

Thrym laughed. "I have more than news. I have the hammer. It is safely hidden and will stay where it is till I get what I want."

Loki asked, "And what do you want?"

"I want the most beautiful goddess to be my wife," said Thrym. "Go to Thor for me and tell him he can have his hammer back as soon as Freya consents to marry me."

When Loki returned to the realm of the gods with this news, Thor felt much relieved to know where his hammer was and that he might get it back.

Thor jumped up at once. "Let us go to Freya. Surely she will consent. Thrym is not too hideous—for a giant."

Once more they marched to the fine, great hall of the goddess of love and beauty. Thor told his good news at once. "We have found my hammer. We know who has it."

Loki added, "And we want to ask you to do us a little favor."

Freya was shaking out the feather flying suit, which they had returned. "You are always asking for something. What is it this time?"

Thor was about to speak, but Loki signaled to him to be quiet. Then Loki began making a fine speech. "We know that you always want to do noble things to help mankind," he said, and went on to give her many compliments. "And now you can get back Thor's hammer and be honored ever afterward."

"Oh?" She seemed skeptical. "And how am I to do that?"

"By marrying Thrym."

She stared at her two guests in astonishment. "Thrym? That horrible old giant?"

"But he has my hammer," Thor pointed out. "And he will not give it back unless you consent to marry him."

"Oh, you miserable, scheming gods!" Freya exclaimed. "Why did I ever come to live among you? Just because you were foolish enough to leave your hammer someplace, you want me to marry a filthy old monster!"

Thor insisted, "I need my hammer to use in fighting the giants."

"Oh, worse and worse!" she cried angrily. "You want me to marry one of your enemies so that you can fight them and me too!"

And the more they pleaded, the angrier she became, until she drove them out of her hall entirely.

When Woden heard of the trouble, he realized at once that it was a matter of great seriousness. He called all the gods and goddesses to meet in solemn assembly.

Several of the gods pleaded with Freya to consent to marry the giant in order for Thor to get back the hammer.

But she waved her arms and shrieked and said she would rather die.

At last keen-eyed Heimdall, the faithful watchman of the gods, stood up among them and spoke. "The solution is easy if we use our wits. Let us dress Thor himself in the white robe of a bride. Let us cover him with a bridal veil and decorate him with a bride's necklace and rings."

"Never!" Thor shouted.

"But it is your hammer," Heimdall pointed out. "You are the one who should go after it."

"Imagine me as a bride!" Thor exclaimed disgustedly.

One after another the gods told him it was a good plan and he ought to try it.

And Woden spoke to him wisely, "Brave Thor, be not overproud. If you do not get back your hammer, you cannot fight the giants. And if you do not fight the giants, they will destroy mankind. You are men's protector. Will you desert them?"

Reluctantly Thor consented.

The gods and goddesses made him a pretty white gown and dressed him as a noble bride. Right joyfully they covered his head with a heavy bridal veil and decorated him with a bride's necklace and rings.

Loki, too, was dressed up. They sewed him a skirt and bonnet like a maidservant. Perhaps he was not very pretty when clothed as a blushing young girl. But he hoped the giants would not know, for it was said they were so ugly themselves they could not tell a cabbage from a rose.

Together the bride and bridesmaid set off in Thor's

164

wagon, which was drawn by two huge goats. In about a week they made the long journey through the mountains to the realm of the giants.

When they came to the first houses a shout of joy greeted them. "Look! Here comes the new bride for Thrym!"

Two of the younger giants ran ahead of them to Thrym's hall, carrying the good news.

When the bride and bridesmaid reached Thrym's hall, he was standing in the doorway to greet them, smiling all over his ugly face and shaking his hands over his head with delight. He clapped the bride such a hearty thump on the back that she stumbled headlong into his hall.

Already the giant had ordered a feast. Thor's eyes under the veil grew bright and his mouth watered as he watched the oxen, sheep, and fish being cooked over the enormous hearth.

Many guests began to arrive, till the vast hall became as noisy as a hurricane merely from the excited, happy chatter of the evil giants. Peeking out through his veil, Thor recognized some of his worst enemies, monsters who had brought many diseases and disasters to man. He especially shuddered at the sight of Thrym's aged sister, as loathesome a witch as ever lived.

When they spoke to him and offered him presents, Thor tried to answer in a light voice and to shake his shoulders and wag his head like a bashful bride. If he did it awkwardly, none of the giants seemed to notice.

But when the food came on the table Thor could not contain the rush of his appetite. He was always a great eater, and now he had not had a good meal for a week, during his hard journey through the mountains.

Reaching out his big hands, he gobbled up eight large salmon. "When is the meal going to begin?" he demanded.

Seeing two servants going by, carrying a whole barbecued ox, he ordered, "Let me taste that!" He wrenched off one piece after another and stuffed them into his mouth. It was so good he ate it all. And he ate all the dainties on the women's table and drank three whole barrels of fermented mead. Then he sighed, looking round for more.

Thrym, his giant host, demanded in astonishment, "Who ever saw a bride with such sharp teeth? Or a maiden who could drink so much?"

Loki, disguised as a bridesmaid, answered cleverly, in a twittering voice, "She was so eager to be with you, she has not eaten for a week!"

By the time most of the guests had finished eating, Thrym had drunk enough himself to be feeling rather tipsy. Leaning across the table, he lifted up the edge of the veil just a little and stuck out his mouth. "Let the bride give me a nice kiss," he rumbled. He raised the veil a little higher. But what he saw made him gape.

The giant leaped back. Turning to the bridesmaid, he demanded, "Why are Freya's eyes so fearful?"

Loki in disguise answered, giving a little simper, "Oh, she was so eager to be with you, she has not slept for a week!"

Following the ancient custom, the bridegroom's sister came to ask the bride for a gift. But Thrym's old sister was such a horrible hag that the bride drew back.

"What is the matter now?" asked the giant.

And Loki answered quickly, "In our country it is the custom for the husband to begin the ceremony by giving his bride a gift. What have you promised to Freya?"

"Oh, ho!" cried Thrym triumphantly. "I have something that will give her joy!" And he called to his servants, "Bring out the hammer!"

Proudly Thrym took the famous hammer in his big hands and laid it on the knees of the bride. "Here is my gift," he boasted, "to bless our marriage. May it bring us many children!"

When Thor saw the hammer lying on his knees, his heart leaped with gladness. For an instant he caressed it with his powerful fingers.

Throwing off the veil, he jumped up and began slaughtering the drunken giants with his fearsome weapon. Thrym's old sister got a knock on the head instead of a bride's gift.

That was how Thor got back his hammer.

Thursday Round the World

Ancient names for Thursday, meaning "planet Jupiter" or "day of Jupiter":

BABYLONIAN	MARDUK
IRANIAN	ORMAZD
GREEK (CULT OF MITHRAS)	ZEUS
SANSKRIT	BRIHASPATIVARA
LATIN	DIES JOVIS
TEUTON	THORSDAG *or* DUNARSDAG (because Thor was often called Dunar, meaning "Thunder")
ICELANDIC	THORSDAGR

The following are modern names. Most have grown from these ancient ones.

From the Latin *dies Jovis* (day of Jupiter):

FRENCH	JEUDI
ITALIAN	GIOVEDI
SPANISH	JEUVES
WELSH	DYDD-IOU

From the Teuton *Thorsdag* and *Dunarsdag*:

ENGLISH	THURSDAY
SWEDISH	TORSDAG
DANISH	TORSDAG
GERMAN	DONNERSTAG
DUTCH	DONDERDAG

THURSDAY

Others meaning "day of the planet Jupiter":

BENGALI	BRIHASPATIBAR
TAMIL	VYAZHA
JAPANESE	MOKUYOBI
ALBANIAN	ENJETE

These mean "fourth day" (which is a mistake) :

RUSSIAN	CHIETVIERG
BULGARIAN	CHETBIARTIAK
POLISH	CZWARTEK
CZECH	CTORTEK
HUNGARIAN	CSORTORTOK
CHINESE	LI-PAI SZE

These mean "fifth day" (which is correct) :

PORTUGUESE	QUINTA-FEIRA
MODERN GREEK	PEMPTI
MODERN ICELANDIC	FIMTUDAGUR
ARABIC	YOM EL HAMYS

And one other:

GAELIC-IRISH	DIAR-DAOIN

("between the fasts"—
because Wednesday
and Friday used to be
fast days)

FRIGG

Friday

WHEN THE Teutons translated the names of the days of
the week, they had no choice for *dies Veneris* (day of the
planet Venus). It had to be Frigg's day.

Of course, Frigg was not the same as Venus. But she
was the only important Teuton goddess.

Venus, in Rome, was the ideal of love and beauty.
Sculptors often modeled beautiful statues of her in the
nude, and her companion was Cupid, who made young
people fall in love with each other. Among the Teutons
the goddess of love and beauty was Freya. Although the
northern climate of the Teutons was too cold for anyone
to go about without clothes, Freya in a nice warm woolen
dress did the best she could to inspire young people with
feelings of romance. Actually she was much needed, for
the young men usually seemed more interested in fighting.

But although Freya was the nearest equivalent the
Teutons had for the goddess Venus, she was only one of
the lesser gods. At the end of the first war between the
real gods and the lesser gods, who were called the Vanir,
Freya had been one of the hostages from the Vanir who
went and lived among the real gods to guarantee that the
war would not start up again. Because she was very lovely
and very friendly, she became popular.

It is true she once refused to do a favor for Thor, when he wanted to get his hammer back by sending her to marry a nasty old giant. She was not willing to be pushed that far. But naturally nobody held that against her.

Still, being only one of the lesser gods and goddesses, she could not be given one of the days of the week.

Frigg was very different, although their names look somewhat alike. In fact, Frigg was also called Frig or Fria or even Frija. But she was not Freya.

Frigg was the goddess of married women. When wives wanted children, they prayed to her. Frigg was also the goddess of medicine and healing. And because she was the wife of the great god Woden, men often prayed to her for help when they were going into battle.

So Friday was named for her.

The Death of the Son of Frigg

Frigg the fair one, wife of Woden, was the mother of a son whom she dearly loved. Cooing over his cradle, she named him Baldr (the Bold Prince) . And she hoped that no harm would fall on his head.

Eagerly she sought out the elements of the earth, all created things, the rocks and rising plants, demanding of each an oath. From iron and from gold and from dreaded bronze she received their promise that never through them would harm come to Baldr. From oak trees and elm and ashwood and hazel the goddess mother had her wish. One after another she canvassed nearly all things, till she grew weary in her search. At last all had promised, save only the mistletoe. That little flowering plant, hanging in trees, she thought too weak to be worth bothering about.

When Baldr grew up, he became the best and handsomest of the gods. Wide-shining was the home of this god of light and of peace, a hall free from all that could be unclean.

And, sure enough, neither stick nor stone nor polished bronze ever harmed him. The other gods for sport threw every sort of weapon at him. Swords, spears, hammers, arrows, and rocks only touched him and fell to the ground as though ashamed and without having given him even a bump.

Then why was he troubled? Why did bad dreams, harsh with foreboding, ride nightly upon the noblest of the gods?

Woden called the council. Anxiously the gods and goddesses met together, but none knew the reason.

Then Woden rose, the old one, skilled in magic enchantment, and laid the saddle on his horse's back. Straight from the home of the blessed he rode down, ever farther down, even to the murky home of Hel, that goddess of the unheroic dead. Here lay both murderers and the innocent murdered, all who did not die fighting.

He knew he was near when he heard the hound. The great watchdog of Hel howled from afar at the father of magic. Near her outer gate Woden met the huge beast. Blood dripped from its jaws and slobbered its chest. But Woden rode forward.

The earth resounded under his horse's hoofs till he reach the tall home of gloom. Woden rode to the eastern door, for there lay the grave of a wise woman, whose fame he knew.

Dismounting in the darkness, Woden bent by the tomb. Magic he spoke and mighty charms, saying the saws, the potent words he had learned from Mimir the water dweller.

So strong was the spell that with a sigh, breaking the ground, the ghost of the wise woman slowly arose.

In death she spoke. "What is the man, to me unknown, that has made me travel the troublesome road? Rough and rat bitten is the path from tomb to air. There have I lain snowed on with snow, smitten with rain, and drenched with dew. Long was I dead. What is your wish?"

Woden answered, "A wanderer am I, and a fighter's son. Speak, I pray you, speak of the realm of Hel, for of heaven I know. For whom are the benches here bright with rings, as for a bridegroom, and the tables of the toothless gay with gold?"

"Here new mead is brewed," she uttered hollowly, "all the best for Baldr. The shining drink waits for him, and a shield lies over it. Let me go. I would return to my earth!"

"Wise woman, cease not!" cried Woden. "Who shall steal the life of Woden's son?"

Sadly she said, "Hoth is bringing the famous branch. 'Tis he shall become the bane of Baldr. I speak unwillingly. Let me be still."

And Woden thought sadly of Hoth.

Hoth was the bitter brother, who had no love for the

handsome hero Baldr. These brothers had been rivals in wooing. They had loved the wonder goddess Nanna. Poor Hoth had been ardent. His longing took away his sleep. Hoth was strong. Heaving his heavy spear, he showed his strength before fair Nanna. She saw only his ill-favored face.

Baldr, the handsome, the hero prince, easily won her. Without even trying, he tied her heart to him.

Their wedding was happy. Only Hoth was not there. In the wild woods he wandered. No one knew what he was feeling.

In an accident while out hunting Hoth was blinded. After that he sat in Frigg's hall. All his strength now useless, he lived on, silent under the eye of his mother. In his bitter heart he held thoughts that could not be spoken. Daily in sunlight he sat, clutching his spear. And often he heaved it, unseeing, into the darkness around him.

Loki, the clever one, god of mischief, entered the hall of Thor one evening and found a feast going on. Woden and Frigg were there. Freya sat at table near Tiu. Many of the great ones were assembled. Only Loki had not been invited.

Sneering, he jeered at the guests.

Thor warned him, "Be silent, Loki. Wise ones know when not to use words."

Loki retorted, naming wittily each weakness or fault

176

of every god present, till at last Thor threw him out into the night.

Next day Loki sought revenge.

In a hilltop field he found the mistletoe. The famous plant looked lovely, full grown at that season. From the branch that seemed too slender and frail Loki fashioned a sharp spear point.

Soon he was whispering in the ear of the silent brother, the strong one, blind Hoth. Loki placed in those hands the dart tipped with mistletoe. And he guided the eyeless one when Baldr passed by.

Nobody thought to cry out a warning, as Hoth hurled. Accustomed to seeing weapons thrown at Baldr and to watching them fall innocently to earth, Frigg only smiled.

But then her smiles ended forever.

Baldr over the hill of death was bowed. And Frigg, wife of Woden, in the Sea Halls was weeping. The wind maidens wept for the shining one and blew up a tempest till ships tossed, their sails flapping to the sky.

With the death of Baldr, god of light and of peace, all that was light and peaceful went out of the world.

Woden had another son to avenge bleeding Baldr. The fierce one, Vali, fought and slew Hoth. His hands he washed not, his hair he combed not, till he had pulled Baldr's foe onto the funeral pyre.

And the gods laid heavy hands on Loki. They bound him in the wet woods, that lover of suffering. Tight to a rock they tied him, and over his head sat a serpent, dripping poison upon him.

By his side his wife Sigyn sat sorrowfully, for even the evil ones love one another. Patiently she held over him a basin to catch the poison. But when it was full and she went to empty it, the poison fell on Loki. Then he thrashed about, causing the earth to shake.

But he was not to sit there forever. At the end of the world, on the day of the doom of the gods, his chains would break.

And this is how that fated day was to come. A giantess was to have a son, another huge wolf. And that wolf would be so big that in the mists of the east one morning he would leap at the sun, take bites out of it, and begin to eat it.

When men saw that, they knew the final day of doom had arrived. All the hours were twilight. The last freezing storm began.

At the dawning of that last day—the day with no sunlight—the watchman of the giants sat on a hill, singing joyously.

Happily he twanged on his harp, while above him the red rooster in the bird wood was crowing, waking the giants for the final struggle.

"To battle!" sang the watchman.

"Ho, ho!" cried the cock. "Bring your swords!"

In Woden's hall the heroes heard Heimdall, the gods' watchman, shout the alarm, while their golden-combed cock crowed.

Deep in the murky valley another cock raised his hoarse voice. It was the dull-red rusty rooster at the barred gate of Hel's home. Her watchdog howled loudly at the cliff-cave mouth. The ghosts of traitors were shaking, quick to fear.

Thus dawned the battle day, the long day of the fate of the gods, those mighty in fight. Brothers would fight and fell each other, and sisters' sons would stain their kinship. Mightily had gods and men lived by the sword. By the same they would perish. War, which they loved, would end all.

The gods at home heard their doom in the shrieking horn held aloft for the loud blast which their watchman blew.

Woden in his hall consulted the wise man's head. Many years he had kept that head embalmed and had fed it. That day the head was long silent. What could it say? At last it gave tongue, "Woden, beware of Fenrir, the wolf you have tied in the wood."

Woden called the gods to council. Eagerly the gods and goddesses sought their places in the assembly.

They could hear dimly in the distance the dwarfs roaring. The hound of Hel was baying. And the wild wolf Fenrir howled as he heaved against his soft, silky chain.

From the east came the giant chief with shield held high. Behind him the mighty marchers, the death-dealers, came thundering. The land of the giants groaned with their footsteps.

From the north on the sea sailed a ship with the people of Hel. Who stood at the tiller? He was Loki. His chain had broken. Now he lead them ashore, the ghosts of murderers, of oath-breakers, of all doers of evil. Wild men with Loki looked for the wolf.

Then the fetters of Fenrir burst. The wolf ran free. The monster, destroyer of gods, sniffed, eager for prey. From mouth to mouth through the forest the news was shouted, "The great wolf is loose!"

All the gods and the brave ghosts of heroes marched to the hard fight. From Valhalla, home of Woden, all warriors who had fought well before, who had been fed and feasted by the Valkyries, had been training for this day. Loyal to the leader, they came, swinging their great swords.

Unafraid, they saw before them the host of the giants, the doers of evil, who hurried from the hills. With a shout, the brave heroes charged.

The giants were staggered. Confused in the shock of the fight, they turned to flee. The heroes cut down the giants like trees in a forest. Like great oaks they thundered to the ground.

Behind the toppling tall ones another fieldful of foe charged. Leading the Vanir, the lesser gods, Loki rushed against heroes and gods. He urged his army. And behind the Vanir the ghosts of Hel were moaning.

The blood-streaked watchdog of Hel was howling. Rushing, reckless with greed, he leaped on the heroes.

One-armed Tiu, bravest of the gods, hurried to rescue them. He aimed his sword at the belly of the enormous beast. But, lacking another arm, Tiu carried no shield. Even as the keen blade slid to his victim's vitals, the teeth of those howling jaws snapped about the brave god.

Two together, like friends embracing, they fell.

Woden went forth to meet the leader of the foe. "Stand and cross swords with me if you dare, treacherous Loki!" he called.

But Loki preferred to rush back into the woods.

He was not gone long. Wearing an evil grin, he returned, beckoning to one behind him.

Then from the deep woods, the thick forest, came Fenrir. The wolf-monster lowered his jaws and slobbered with greed, searching the army of gods and heroes. Suddenly he threw up his head. He had sighted Woden. The huge wolf roared. His muscles bulged as he sprang to the attack.

Woden stood ready. His sword slashed forth. For a moment the wolf drew away.

Again the heavy monster sprang to the attack. Woden wielded his sword. But suddenly Loki with a stout spear knocked aside the sword of Woden. The wolf's teeth gnashed the god.

Woden's wife, Frigg the fair one, hurried to his side. Then was her hour to weep.

Woden's son Vithar galloped up on his horse. To fight for his father he had left his home, that land filled with growing trees and high-standing grass. The son leaped down from his steed to avenge his father. Vithar was famed for his big shield too heavy for others to wield. With his great strength he raised his heavy sword to fight the foaming wolf.

Fenrir roared greedily, eager for flesh.

Loki jeered, "Thou, too?"

But Woden's son thrust his sword into the huge wolf straight to the heart.

Nearby stood Thor. To Loki he said, "I, too, am kin of high Woden. Do you laugh now?" He heaved his hammer.

Loki harmed no one any more.

Thor hurled his hammer again and again at the foe. The lightning-flash flared as the Vanir were felled. But then came the forest fire, destroyer of branches. And the faces of foemen glowed red in the battle.

Through the flaming forest the writhering snake wriggled, the great girdler of ocean, the Midgard Serpent. His breath was a mist of poison. Before him the heroes were falling.

In anger great Thor, the watchman of the world, strode forward fearlessly. In nine paces he came before the great snake.

"Hold!" cried he. "You have slain enough. Now be gone!"

"Sweet is the sight of thee," hissed the serpent. "We two shall decide the issue of war. Fall, Thor, forever!" The serpent lunged forward. His huge, evil head shone in the smoky murk, his great jaws agape.

With sure aim Thor hurled his hammer at its head. Sinking, the monster gasped its last breath.

Thor turned. But he staggered in the mist from the snake's nostrils. The fearful poison, floating on air, felled him. Mightily he crashed to the ground.

The flames grew fiercer. All the world was burning. The twilight of the gods was reddened by the final bonfire. Melting in the heat, the whole earth shuddered and sank staggeringly into the sea.

Down fell the hot stars, whirled from heaven. With their white-glowing heat, the huge ocean boiled. Fierce grew the steam, rising higher and higher.

Bravely they had fought to the very end, all the war-loving ones, the mighty in fight.

Friday Round the World

Ancient names for Friday meaning "planet Venus" or "day of Venus":

BABYLONIAN	ISHTAR
IRANIAN	ANAHITA
GREEK (CULT OF MITHRAS)	APHRODITE
SANSKRIT	SUKRAVARA
LATIN	DIES VENERIS
TEUTON	FRIGADAG *or* FRIADAG
ICELANDIC	FRIADAGR

The following are modern names. Most have grown from these ancient ones.

From the Latin *dies Veneris:*

FRENCH	VENDREDI
ITALIAN	VENERDI
SPANISH	VIERNES
WELSH	DYDD-GWENER

From the Teuton *Friadag:*

ENGLISH	FRIDAY
GERMAN	FREITAG
DUTCH	VRIJDAG
SWEDISH	FREDAG
DANISH	FREDAG

These also mean "day of Venus":

BENGALI	SUKRABAR
TAMIL	VELLI
JAPANESE	KINYOBI

This means "day of the evening star":

ALBANIAN	PREMTE

These mean "fifth day" (which is a mistake):

RUSSIAN	PIATNEETSA
BULGARIAN	PETIAK
POLISH	PIATEK
CZECH	PATEK
HUNGARIAN	PENTEK
CHINESE	LI-PAI WU

This means "sixth day" (which is correct):

PORTUGUESE	SEXTA-FEIRA

These mean "fast day":

MODERN ICELANDIC	FOESTUDAGUR
GAELIC-IRISH	DI-H-AOINE

Others:

MODERN GREEK	PARASKEVI ("preparation day")
ARABIC	YOM EL GUM'A ("assembly day" because Friday is the Moslem day for religious worship)

On Fridays Catholics must not eat meat. The earliest Christians adopted this taboo because of a very ancient idea that people ought to do without some pleasure at least one day a week.

Some old customs made Friday seem unlucky. It was remembered as the day of the crucifixion. And in the Middle Ages it was hangman's day, when crowds came to watch people being hanged. When anyone had a gloomy expression, his neighbors said he had a "Friday look"—as though he were going to be hanged. But the reason why English schoolboys used to call it "black Friday" was simply that the end of the week was the day for examinations.

SATURN

Saturday

WHEN THE Teutons translated the names of the days of the week into their language, they were really stumped by the last one, *dies Saturni*. "The day of Saturn?" they asked. "Who is Saturn?"

Saturn was the most distant planet (the most distant known at that time). It was the slow traveler.

They had never heard of it.

Saturn, also, was a Roman god of seed planting and farming.

That did not help. The Teutons looked down their noses at farming. They went hunting. They herded cattle and reindeer. They had a few slaves who planted a vegetable garden now and then. At that time (A.D. 100 to 200) farming, among the Teutons, was not an honored profession. They could not imagine having an important god connected with it.

Rather contemptuously some of them pronounced the Latin name as best they could and made a word out of it in their own language: *Saeternesdag*. But only a couple of tribes consented to say this. Therefore the word survives now only in English and Dutch. Most of the Teutonic tribes called it "bath day."

Who was this Saturn, whom the Teutons could not understand?

189

The God of Seeds

The main occupation in Italy was farming. Rich people and poor tilled the soil, both gentlemen and slaves. The best poets wrote long books on how to trim your vines and when to plant or reap. Even in very early times —long before the Romans had any empire—farming had been so important that the people had had several gods for it.

Saturn was originally the god of the planting. His name was made from *satus* (seed) . He was supposed to protect the seed after it had been sowed. And when people said prayers to him, they were worshiping the mysterious forces that make the seed come to life and begin to grow under the earth.

Those forces of life are still rather mysterious. When you are planting a garden or even a flowerpot, do you look sometimes at a seed and wonder how that tiny thing can contain within itself the secret of life and also the whole pattern of the plant it is going to be—with its roots, its stems, its many leaves, its blossoming flowers that will nod in the breeze some sunny day, and then its fruit and seeds, perhaps hundreds of them—all from this one seed which you are about to place in the earth?

As Italy was a warm country, the farmers plowed in October and planted in November. Through the winter the crops grew slowly.

In April the buds began to open. Then came the season of the goddess Ceres, protectress of the standing grain. (Her name gives us our word *cereal*.)

When it was ripe in the early summer, the reapers prayed to Ops, goddess of the wealth of the harvest. (Her name gives us our word *opulent*.)

Many other deities, both good and evil, hung over the fields. For instance, the farmers prayed also to Lua, the vile one, goddess of plague, fire, and destruction. They begged her to stay away. Sometimes soldiers (having been brought up on farms), after winning a battle, would gather the enemy shields, helmets, spears, arrows, and other weapons into a heap and burn them for the vile goddess.

"Take these, O Lua," they would pray, "and be satisfied, and leave our fields alone."

Saturn, of course, was the enemy of this dreaded Lua. Some people said his wife was Ops, the goddess of the harvest.

He was pictured as a wise old man with a long beard. He carried a curved knife, with which to cut the grain and prune the fruit trees and trim the vines. Or sometimes he carried a scythe.

As time passed, people added new jobs for him.

He became the god of dung piles and fertilizer—very important to farmers.

And then he became the Romans' Santa Claus, the

jolly god of gift giving. His holiday, the Saturnalia, was their Christmas. So the poets made up a story to explain that holiday.

The Story of Saturn

One day a beautiful ship appeared at the mouth of the Tiber River and began to sail inland among the wild expanses of forest. The savage people who lived in that region had never seen such a thing. So they ran to the banks of the river to watch.

Two days' journey upstream good King Janus ruled as best he could in his town, Janiculum, built on a hill by the river. But his task was hard, and he often felt discouraged, because his people were utterly wild and ignorant. They fished and hunted and squabbled with one another. They were terribly poor and always in trouble.

When the mysterious, beautiful ship arrived at Janiculum, King Janus hurried to the shore. A brave king, surrounded by his huntsmen, he was not afraid of one sailboat, even though he had never seen such a thing before. And when a sad, dignified old man with a long beard stood up in the ship and looked back at him with sorrowful eyes, Janus called out, "Welcome to our kingdom, stranger! Come ashore, and be my guest."

After he had led the wise-looking old stranger up to

the town and they were seated at table and served with fish and meat, the king asked, "Tell us, stranger, what is your name, and from what land do you come voyaging so sadly in your marvelous ship?"

In a deep voice the traveler replied, "In your tongue let my name be called Saturn, for I see that your men do not know how to plant seeds, nor do they understand the mysteries of plowing and reaping. All this will I teach you. Then you shall be poor no longer but shall enjoy abundance of food and merriment throughout the winter season."

Janus and his men were very much pleased to hear this. Respectfully they waited to hear more.

After a pause the traveler continued, "But in my own country I was known as Father Cronus, and I was ruler of that land." And he told the exciting story of his rise to power and how he fell.

In Greece, by driving out his father, who had been king before him, Cronus became king. Then long and well did Cronus rule.

But he had one aching fear. A prophecy had said that just as he had driven out his father, so also one of his own children would some day drive him into exile.

So when his wife had babies, fear took hold of his wits. Not knowing what else to do with his children to prevent them from someday fighting against him, he swallowed them, one by one. Five he swallowed. But the sixth escaped, for Cronus' wife tricked him, giving him a big stone to thrust into his mouth instead.

The son who escaped was the strongest, young Zeus. He grew up on a distant island, the bravest god who had ever lived. When he was full grown he went on purpose to the palace to see his father, the great swallower. And Zeus gave him a powerful medicine, which caused Cronus to open his huge mouth, and all five young gods came leaping out.

Then Zeus and his brothers made war on Father Cronus and drove him from the country.

(This is a little different from the story the Greeks told of the rise of Zeus the Thunderer. This is the Roman version of it.)

"But now that I am here," the bearded traveler concluded, "let my name be called Saturn, for I will give your people seeds and will teach you the way to wealth and happiness."

Next day Saturn called the people of Janiculum around him and began their lessons. Janus and his huntsmen were eager pupils, for they had been deeply impressed by the wisdom and goodness of the mysterious old stranger.

First Saturn (as they agreed to call him) taught them how to plant the sacred seeds of wheat and also beans and other good things to eat.

Then he taught those student farmers the use of dung for fertilizing their fields.

And he showed them how to gather bees and train these insects to swarm in the hive, and how to extract the honey from the golden honeycomb.

King Janus was so much pleased by all this knowledge that he summoned the assembly of his chief men and in their presence spoke solemnly to their wisdom-giving guest.

"Noble Saturn, let my name be remembered in aftertimes as the king who was not ungrateful to you in your hour of sadness. For you arrived among us a refugee, driven from your homeland, and here you have rewarded our hospitality by teaching us the most important wisdom, which we see will soon make us wealthy and strong. Therefore I will give you a suitable present in return —even half my kingdom. Here on this hill beside the river we call our city Janiculum. On the other side of the river you see that other fair hill. Take now whichever of my men are pleasing in your sight, and go to that hill. There you may build a city of your own, and rule over it as king. And together we shall share dominion over the whole countryside."

Smiling at last, Saturn gave him many thanks. And when he had selected a party of able men, he marched off with them. Cheering, they crossed the river, climbed the hill, and set their hands to the happy task.

Soon they had built such a fine city that it was called the Capitol. And the hill is still known as the Capitoline Hill even to this day.

When the grain had been harvested, Saturn taught his people the arts of cooking.

As the years passed, the kingdom became fat with the produce of the land. Janus and Saturn were not like later kings but were so wise that they ruled side by side without ever fighting.

To help keep the people peaceful Janus used to remind them of their bitter past, full of misery and quarrels. "See how much better off you are now, with plenty to eat and fine clothes to wear. Remember to show your gratitude by being peaceful with one another."

The people were impressed by his knowledge of the past and also by his foresight. They said, "He must have foreseen all this ease and plenty. That is why he welcomed the stranger in the first place."

And so the legend grew up that Janus had two faces, one for looking behind and one for looking ahead.

The kingdom became so prosperous that the market places were crammed with useful things, which people bought and sold. For money they used little sticks of silver or copper. But as these were of all different sizes, every merchant had to have a scale and weigh them carefully. Making change was extremely difficult.

But Saturn gave them another invention. He taught them how to stamp coins. The first coins had a picture of his head on one side, and on the other side a boat, because he had arrived in one. For many centuries after-

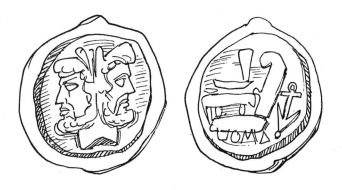

ward when children tossed any coin they cried out, "Head or boat?" (When coins went to England this expression was changed to "heads or tails.")

And Saturn taught them how to build ships and sail them, so that they could exchange their goods with distant nations.

He showed them how to train fruit trees and the art of grafting part of one plant onto another, to produce better peaches or plums.

And he gave them laws and taught them the art of governing.

But when all was going well, one day great Saturn disappeared. He simply vanished. In the morning he went out to oversee the work in the fields. That afternoon he was nowhere to be seen. Though the farmers searched for many days, they found no trace of him.

Janus then called his people together and told them, "Although our beloved Saturn has left us, his memory will stay with us always. Let us build an altar to him and worship him as a god, for he is one who has improved the condition of life."

The citizens cheered with approval, for they said, "From heaven he came to us, and to heaven he has returned."

And Janus told them, "Great Saturn came to us on the seventeenth of December, bringing his gifts of wisdom which have made us happy. Therefore let us hold a joyous

Saturnalia every year on that day, when we shall give gifts to one another in memory of his gifts to us."

So the Saturnalia was begun. Gradually it became the year's most popular festival.

When good King Janus died, people built an altar to him, too. Because he had ruled over a city of peaceful homes, they said he was the protector of doorways. They made little statues of him with two faces and set him to guard their houses.

Afterward there was no limit to what the poets would say about how wonderful life used to be in the age of Saturn.

Vergil's *Aeneid*, which students of Latin read in high school, tells the story with the greatest affection. Some said that in that Golden Age nobody had to work: crops grew by themselves. The poets put in everything they wished they could see. No house had doors—because there were no thieves. No merchants sent men on dangerous voyages in search of profit. People did not need gold, for the fields yielded crops so abundantly that everyone had plenty.

Then there were no armies, no lust for blood, no battles. No swords were made by the cruel armorer's ruthless skill.

Even religion was better then. Farmers said a few simple prayers and dealt respectfully with their neighbors, instead of having long-winded, elaborate ceremonies with expensive altars and fancy costumes of gold and jewels, as they do nowadays (says Vergil, writing in the year 25 B.C.).

Another poet adds that thunderbolts did not strike people so often in those days. And there were not so many people who deserved to be struck!

Above all, in those days (all the poets agreed) people were not divided into social ranks: the kings and princes, the nobles, the common people, and then the slaves. In Saturn's Golden Age anyone could hold his head up in anybody's presence, because all the people had equal rights.

Io Saturnalia!

If you go to Rome you can see the ruins of the Temple of Saturn and Ops in the Forum. It is at the foot of the Capitoline Hill, the same hill on which Saturn was said to have built his city in the distant days of legend. In fact, the back of the temple is right against the steep cliff of that hill.

It used to be a handsome building, with an altar in the middle and a space out front where the whole Roman Senate could meet. Up near the roof, at the front, were statues of Tritons. They were sea gods with tails like fish, and they were shown blowing loudly on horns made of conch shells, to direct the winds (because the story said Saturn had arrived in a ship).

Down below was a huge statue of Saturn, shown as an old, bearded man—like Santa Claus. But Saturn had a sickle stuck in his belt. The feet of the statue were tied with soft ropes made of wool, to keep him from running away (because the story said he had walked off one day and disappeared). But on the days of his festival, the Saturnalia, these ropes were untied.

In the days of Caesar and Vergil this temple was not used much for religious ceremonies. But it was used. The Senators, who came there in their dressy white togas, kept the state treasure in it. And in a back room, cut in the rock of the hill, they kept the official copies of the laws. (Rome became head of a big empire with many laws, and this room was rather large.)

The Senators invented theories about why they kept the money there. They said, for instance, that they did it because in Saturn's day there had been no thieves. A more practical reason was that the thieves of Rome actually had a superstition against stealing from Saturn. (It would be like stealing from Santa Claus.)

During most of the year the people did not bother to worship Saturn (just as we do not talk much about Santa Claus in April or July).

But at seed-planting time (in November) some of the farmers remembered to pray to him.

And when the planting was finished and his day arrived, all Rome seemed to go wild. That was the time for parties and for giving gifts. (Scholars say it was the origin of our custom of giving gifts at Christmas.)

On the 17th of December the festivities began fairly solemnly. A parade of government officials marched to the Forum, where they performed an open-air sacrifice of cattle in front of Saturn's temple. Then a feast was served out of doors in the Forum for the Senators and some of the other dignitaries. During this part of the celebration they wore their formal white togas.

But when this meal ended, they took off these formal clothes, put on less dressy shirts and leggings, and departed shouting, "Io Saturnalia!" (Hail to the Saturnalia!).

Other people were waiting eagerly to hear this cry. As soon as it began, everyone who heard it shouted it. So it very quickly ran all across the city. It was like our greeting "Merry Christmas"—but more noisy.

Then almost everyone put on what they called Liberty Caps—the same peaked Phrygian caps the revolutionists wore much later in the French Revolution—and familiar as the cap that Mithras wore. Even slaves, who were forbidden to cover their heads at any other time during the year, gaily put on these holiday hats.

The slaves then ran out into the streets, yelling with joy. For a few days they were temporarily free. As one poet expressed it, "In cap-glad Rome the slave, as he rattles the dice box, has no fear of the police officer." The rest of the year they were forbidden to gamble.

The free people enjoyed themselves too. Another poet wrote, "The days of the Saturnalia, the best of days!"

The 18th and 19th of December began with early

baths (your choice of hot or cold). The Romans loved baths. They built huge buildings where anyone with even a little money could go and bathe, read in a library, listen to music, and talk with his friends. These great buildings were crowded during the holidays.

At noon came the family feast. The traditional main course (if you could afford it, for it was expensive) was a roasted little pig—very tender. After the meal the children and their parents went to call on friends. They greeted everyone with, "Io Saturnalia!" They congratulated their friends on anything pleasant that had happened. Then they gave gifts and spent the afternoon playing games.

On the evenings of these days the families got together for larger parties. Then the slaves sat at table with their masters and could say whatever they chose, like free people.

Often they made jokes about their masters. And the masters had to get up and bring the food from the kitchen and serve the slaves.

People said this custom was in memory of Saturn's Golden Age, when there had been no masters and no slaves, for all had had equal rights.

Originally the Saturnalia had been only one day. But gradually through the years it became so popular that it was extended to two, three, five, and at last seven days! All government offices and law courts were closed.

Schools were on holiday. The officials would not declare a war or execute a criminal during those days of joy.

When Augustus was emperor he cut it down a little. He decreed that during the Saturnalia the government offices would not be closed for more than three days.

One of the poets—Martial—has left us a list of the gifts that people used to give. It really is amazing.

One traditional present to give was a wax candle—because this was the shortest day of the year, when candles were offered to the sun, begging it to come back again. (Actually the Roman calendar was not very accurate, as the Romans had never known much about astronomy; so the day of the Saturnalia slipped away from the shortest day. Around the year 20 B.C. they realized that it was off and tried moving the Saturnalia from December 17 to 19, but that was still wrong, for the shortest day at that time was December 25.)

The other traditional present to give was a little clay doll. During the days of the Saturnalia roadside booths were set up all over Rome, where these dolls were sold. They were like our Christmas cards and were made in all shapes and colors.

Children spent a long time choosing the ones they liked, and then gave them to their friends, who received them with shouts of joy. (Like Christmas cards, they were thrown away soon afterward.)

If you had money you might give more expensive pres-

205

ents. The poet Martial lists some he had received: good napkins, elegant shoe fastenings, wax writing tablets, and a nice vase filled with sugared plums. Children liked sugared plums, but Martial was sick of them and made a lot of jokes about them. He used to say that when you ran out of ideas for a present to give, you could always give sugared plums. And he wrote a letter to a wealthy but stingy man:

"You sent eight tall Syrian slaves, in handsome uniforms, to bring me your present of worthless feathers and baskets of sugared plums—all of which you had received as presents the day before. It would have been less trouble for you and more fun for me if you had just sent one slave in his ordinary working clothes, to bring me some silver coins."

Then a friend asked Martial to help him out with his Saturnalia list.

Martial suggested, if a man wanted to give presents to his friends and relatives, why not send a handsome parchment copy of the *Iliad* or the *Odyssey?* Or write a poem yourself and send it. Or, better still, just send a blank sheet of parchment with no poem on it (especially if it was a very bad poem).

Or send a puppy, a pony, a greyhound, a monkey, or even a mule. Or a pig. Or just some sausages. Another good present would be a parrot, a magpie, a nightingale, or a hawk. If you don't like the person, send him a crow. Or if you can't find a bird, send an empty birdcage. Or you can always send candied plums.

Martial's friend had plenty of money. He might give a slave. For instance, a buffoon, a clown, or a dancer. Or, better still, a shorthand writer. (Martial, writing about the year A.D. 70, describes in detail how the shorthand writer writes faster than you can talk.) Or, if you don't want to spend that much, give a pair of cymbals, a flute, a drum, reed pipes, or a lyre, so that the person to whom you are giving this present can amuse himself. Or, if you're stingy, give just a pluck for a lyre.

Have you a nephew who is an athlete? Give him a football or a handball stuffed with feathers, a pair of dumb-bells, an athlete's leather cap, a sweat-scraper, a flask of skin oil, or a horsewhip. Or, if he has been misbehaving again, give him a baby's rattle.

Martial was sure that some of your friends would appreciate nice ivory boxes—or carved wooden ones—or a pair of dice, a gaming table, a pen case, an ivory toothpick, an ear pick, or a back scraper in the shape of a hand. A broad-brimmed hat was always welcome, or hunting spears, a hunting knife, a sword and belt, a dagger, a scythe, a hatchet, or why not a set of barber's instruments?

If you're thinking of a lady, have you thought of a gold hairpin, some combs, a parasol? Maybe she would like some hair dye. Hm? Or just some tooth powder.

Everyone gives candles. Now, candlesticks are good for a change, especially fancy ones made of bronze or gold. Or you might give a lantern enclosed with thin sheets of horn.

Woolen slippers were Martial's favorite. Or a fly-chaser made of peacock's feathers. Or a toga, a warm cloak, a cloak with a hood, a dinner shirt, or even a pair of socks. Oh, he could think of lots of nice things! A pillow, a blanket, a rug, a mattress stuffed with wool, or with reeds, or with feathers—or even with hay. A bell for your friend's servant to ring when his bath was ready. Or an iron tire for his chariot wheel.

Of course, if you wanted to be really thoughtful, you could give a strainer with which to strain snow when putting it into wine.

Not just a linen strainer. A special silk one. Oh, well, a linen one would do. Or a jug, or a wine cup of crystal. Or a cup trimmed with jewels. A pitcher for snow water. Or just give your friend some snow.

Or sugared plums?

Martial says a young boy was eagerly expecting a present from his friend. He waited all through the Saturnalia, and nothing arrived. So the boy wrote his friend a letter: "I waited five days for your present, and nothing arrived. All right for you! Next year that's exactly the present you will receive from me!"

Saturday Round the World

Ancient names meaning "planet Saturn" or "day of Saturn":

BABYLONIAN	NINURTA
IRANIAN	KEVAN
GREEK (CULT OF MITHRAS)	CRONUS
SANSKRIT	SANIVARA
LATIN	DIES SATURNI

From the Latin *dies Saturni:*

ANCIENT TEUTON	SAETERNESDAG
ENGLISH	SATURDAY
DUTCH	ZATERDAG
WELSH	DYDD-SADWRN
GAELIC-IRISH	DI-SATHIRNE *or* DIA SATHUIRN
ALBANIAN	SHTUNE

Others from Mithraism (these mean "bath day"):

SWEDISH	LOERDAG
DANISH	LOERDAG
MODERN ICELANDIC	LAUGARDAGUR

Other modern names meaning "day of Saturn":

BENGALI	SANIBAR
TAMIL	SANI
JAPANESE	DOYOBI

The ancient Hebrew word was *Shabbath* (day of rest). From it these words were made:

SEVEN DAYS FROM SUNDAY

ANCIENT GREEK (CHRISTIANS AND JEWS)	SABBATON
LATIN (CHRISTIANS AND JEWS)	DIES SABBATI
OLD ENGLISH	SABAT
MODERN ENGLISH	SABBATH
FRENCH	SAMEDI (from the vulgar Latin *Sambati*)
ITALIAN	SABATO
SPANISH	SABADO
PORTUGUESE	SABADO
MODERN GREEK	SAVATO
RUSSIAN	SOOBBOTA
POLISH	SOBOTA
CZECH	SOBOTA
BULGARIAN	SIABOTA
HUNGARIAN	SZOMBAT
ARABIC	YOM ES SABT

Others:

GERMAN	SONNABEND ("eve of Sunday")
CHINESE	LI-PAI LIU ("of the week, six")

If you try to translate "Sunday is the Sabbath" into French or any language down to Arabic, you can't. In Spanish, for instance, *"El domingo es el sabado"* means "Sunday is Saturday," which is nonsense.

Index

Sunday, 95; Monday, 113; Wednesday, 143; Thursday, 169; Friday, 186; Saturday, 210

Icelandic language, days in, 68: Sunday, 94; Monday, 112; Tuesday, 79, 128, 129; Wednesday, 79, 142, 143; Thursday, 79, 168, 169; Friday, 79, 185, 186; Saturday, 79, 85, 209
India (*see also* Sanskrit), 78
Iran, Mithraism in, 26-30
Iranian language, days in: Sunday, 94; Monday, 112; Tuesday, 128; Wednesday, 142; Thursday, 168; Friday, 185; Saturday, 209
Ishtar, Babylonian goddess, 10
Isis, cult of, 33, 64, 68-69, 71, 73
Italian language, days in: Sunday, 95; Monday, 112; Tuesday, 128; Wednesday, 142; Thursday, 168; Friday, 185; Saturday, 210
Italy, *see* Roman Empire

Japan, the week of, 2, 79
Japanese language, days in: Sunday, 95; Monday, 113; Tuesday, 129; Wednesday, 143; Thursday, 169; Friday, 186; Saturday, 209
Jesus Christ, 87, 88, 90
Jupiter: hours named for, 18-21; in Mithraism, 63, 65, 67-68;

religion of, 10, 75, 115; Thursday named for, 22, 145

Karnak, temple of, 4

Latin, days in: Sunday, 94; Monday, 112; Tuesday, 128; Wednesday, 142; Thursday, 168; Friday, 185; Saturday, 209, 210
Loki, Teutonic god, 66, 148-149, 159-167, 176-183

Marduk, Babylonian god, 10, 15
Mars: hours named for, 18-21; in Mithraism, 63, 67, 68; religion of, 10, 75; Tuesday named for, 22, 115-116
Martial, Roman poet, 205-208
Mercury: hours named for, 18-21; in Mithraism, 63, 68; religion of, 10, 75; Wednesday named for, 22, 131
Mithraism: names of gods in, 65-68; religion of, 26-34, 60-64, 68-78; and Sunday, 81, 83-85
Mithras, god of light, 26-28, 31, 34, 35-59, 62, 76-78, 84
Monday: history of, 75, 97-113; name of, 22; number of, 92; translations of, 112-113
month, measurement of, 4, 13-15, 22, 63, 98-111
moon: eclipse of, 105; hours named for, 18-21; measurement by the, 4, 98-111; in Mithraism, 50, 62; Monday named for, 22, 97; movement

INDEX

ABOUT THE AUTHOR

Tom Galt, historian and biographer, was born in Michigan and brought up in St. Louis. He was graduated from Harvard in the class of 1932; and he then joined the staff of the Ethical Culture School at Fieldston in New York, where for eight years he was a librarian and teacher.

Now Mr. Galt devotes all of his working time to writing, and he lives and studies quietly in New York. But between books he and his wife are usually on the road or in the air, for they both love to travel and delight in the art museums, the music, and the theaters of each country they visit. Because Mr. Galt is an accomplished linguist he is able to indulge his hobbies to the full, whether he is in London, Paris, Rome, or Mexico City.

In addition to his writing, Mr. Galt has lectured widely on economics and international relations. Three summers spent in Mexico resulted in the writing of several pamphlets for the Pan-American Union and his first book for children, entitled *Volcano*. Other books followed, and each of them has been translated into many different languages. Mr. Galt can visit India, Japan, Iceland, or Scandinavia and find his books in the schools and libraries.